GET THE RIGHT JOB IN 60 DAYS OR LESS

RICHARD H. BEATTY

John Wiley & Sons, Inc.

New York • Chichester • Brisbane • Toronto • Singapore

In recognition of the importance of preserving what has
been written, it is a policy of John Wiley & Sons, Inc.
to have books of enduring value published in the United
States printed on acid-free paper, and we exert our best
efforts to that end.

Copyright © 1991 by John Wiley & Sons, Inc.

This publication is designed to provide accurate and
authoritative information in regard to the subject
matter covered. It is sold with the understanding that
the publisher is not engaged in rendering legal, accounting,
or other professional service. If legal advice or other
expert assistance is required, the services of a competent
professional person should be sought. *From a Declaration
of Principles jointly adopted by a Committee of the
American Bar Association and a Committee of Publishers.*

Library of Congress Cataloging in Publication Data

Beatty, Richard H.. 1939-
  Get the right job in 60 days or less / by Richard H. Beatty.
    p.   cm.
  Includes bibliographical references.
  ISBN: 0471-52612-6 (cloth). — ISBN 0-471-52613-4 (pbk.)
  1. Job hunting.   I. Title.
  HF5382.7.B44   1991
  650.14—dc20   90-25246

Printed in the United States of America

91 92 10 9 8 7 6 5 4 3 2

*To those who wish
to improve their job-hunting skills
and learn creative ways
to expedite their job search.*

PREFACE

Why is it that one person can find a job in only 6 or 8 weeks while another, with substantially similar qualifications, will require 6 to 8 months? Also, why is it that one major out-placement consulting firm reports that its clients take an average of 7.2 months to find employment, while another reports that it averages only 3.2 months (less than half the time of the first firm)?

These differences aren't accidental—they don't just "happen." Obviously, the faster group is conducting its job search much differently. Put simply, it knows something that the slower group does not and is doing some things the slower group isn't.

What are the secrets of a speedy job search? What can be learned from the experiences of other successful job seekers who have found the right job quickly? What do the employment experts say about sources and techniques that can help you short-cut your job search and reach your employment goals quickly?

These are the questions answered by this book. Statistical evidence is cited for the use of certain employment sources and techniques that are "known" to be the critical building blocks of efficient job search strategies. Knowing about and effectively using these methods can clearly take the trial-and-error out of job-hunting, replace it with "proven" methods that work, and shave valuable time from the job-hunting campaign.

This book provides a step-by-step recipe for conducting a fast and effective job search. It starts by identifying the most productive job-hunting sources and, with supporting statistical evidence, shows that <u>only 3 employment sources</u> (out of hundreds from which you can choose) account for <u>92% of all jobs found.</u> Why then waste valuable time and effort on the hundreds of other sources that produce only 8% of the results?

If you are committed to conducting a successful and speedy job search, simply knowing which 3 of these sources produce 92% of the employment results is in itself not enough. This book, therefore, closely examines each of these key sources individually, and offers step-by-step strategies for exploiting the full potential of each. This includes special shortcuts, tricks, and techniques that have historically translated into meaningful time savings for the job seeker.

This book has been written as a step-by-step guide for the job seeker who wishes to conduct a short, hard-hitting job-hunting campaign. The aim is to provide the reader with <u>a very specific plan</u> for conducting a successful job search in 60 days or less. It therefore leads the reader methodically through each step of the way, showing what sources to focus on, what methods and techniques to use, and when and how to use them for maximum results and effectiveness.

Besides the core chapters on critical employment sources and time-saving job-hunting techniques, the reader is also furnished with a "how to" chapter that completely covers the preparation of modern employment resumes, including samples. In the final chapter, the reader is also introduced to "power interview strategies"—unique approaches that can provide the reader with a substantial competitive advantage in conducting a successful employment interview.

This book provides a complete and well-documented prescription for conducting an efficient job-hunting campaign. The techniques presented here have already been used by others to cut months off their job search. It is my firm belief that by carefully following the step-by-step plan offered here, most readers will be able to cut their job search time in half (or better). For many, finding the right job in 60 days or less will clearly be an achievable goal.

My best wishes for a very successful job search and a highly rewarding, satisfying career!

Richard H. Beatty
West Chester, Pennsylvania

CONTENTS

CHAPTER 1

THE 60-DAY CONCEPT
How to Streamline Your
Job-Hunting Campaign
1

CHAPTER 2

BEST SOURCES
FOR FINDING A JOB
What the Studies Show
9

CHAPTER 3

RESUME POWER
Getting the Most From
Your Employment Resume
21

CHAPTER 4

DIRECT MAIL
How to "Jump Start" Your Job Search
45

ix

CHAPTER 5

TAPPING THE FULL POWER
OF RECRUITMENT ADVERTISING
63

CHAPTER 6

THE STRONG CASE FOR NETWORKING
What the Experts Say
79

CHAPTER 7

GETTING PAST THE SECRETARY
91

CHAPTER 8

THE NETWORKING PHONE CALL
131

CHAPTER 9

THE GREAT NETWORKING SHORTCUT
How To Cut 75% from Job Search Time
169

CHAPTER 10

POWER STRATEGIES
FOR SUCCESSFUL INTERVIEWS
187

INDEX

195

CHAPTER 1

THE 60-DAY CONCEPT

How To Streamline Your Job-Hunting Campaign

Yes, there will be skeptics! There will be some who will pick up this book and say, "It can't be done. It's not possible to find the right job in 60 days or less." For them, the idea of job search and time savings is an incompatible and mutually exclusive concept. For them the pairing of these terms is an oxymoron.

To these skeptics and doubting Thomas's, my answer is quite simple: "Not only can it be done, but I've seen it done." (In fact, our firm recently counseled an individual who sucessfully applied the techniques presented in this book and found a job in only 37 work days.) What is more, I firmly believe that with the right job search strategy, some good coaching, a little determination, and reasonable effort, the average job seeker can, and will, achieve the 60-day objective with consistency.

To the rest of you—the curious, the open-minded—I am here to offer some hope and encouragement. I offer not just the "emotional support" necessary to carry out an effective (and time-efficient) job search, but the "specific methodology" as well. To you I offer (through the subsequent chapters of this book) a step-by-step recipe for cutting considerable time off your job search and still finding the job you seek.

What I am prescribing in this book is a step-by-step, integrated strategy for job hunting that embodies the best known sources and techniques for finding a job. This is statistically sound methodology that has proven, over time, to produce the very best job-hunting results. Additionally, it should allow you to shave considerable time from your job-hunting campaign.

Will this plan work for everyone? Can anyone, using this approach, expect to find a job in 60 days or less? Quite frankly, the answer is "no." But it will work for the great majority of you, if you are willing to work hard and give it a try. It is based upon sound, proven sources and methods that can, and will, stack the deck substantially in your favor!

THE 60-DAY CONCEPT

What is the 60-day concept? How does it work? Why will it cut substantial time off my search?

Although this book is intended to provide detailed answers to these questions, I will (in this chapter) at least share with you the underlying concepts that are the basis for the success of this 60-day job search strategy.

The underlying principles upon which this book is written are quite simple. They are as follows:

1. *Need to identify the* best *job search sources*
    Focusing your job search on the *best* job sources (that is, the ones that have *statistically* proven to produce the most jobs) will cut significant time from the job search process.

2. *Need to eliminate* nonproductive *job search sources*
    Eliminating *nonproductive* sources—those that are *statistically* known to produce few or no jobs—from the job search will save considerable job search time.

3. *Need to prioritize the* best *job search sources*
    Prioritizing the *best* job search sources (those statistically shown to produce the most jobs) provides a further basis for greater efficiency and improved job search time utilization.

4. *Need to exploit each* best *source fully*
    Effective, efficient job search requires that you be well-trained in the methods and techniques that will allow you to fully exploit the best employment sources.

Overall, then, the key to conducting effective and time-efficient job search is choosing the most productive sources and using them well. Choice of the wrong sources, coupled with ineffective use of these sources, clearly has the potential to add several additional months to the job-hunting process.

KEY BARRIERS TO AN EFFECTIVE JOB SEARCH

Most well-meaning job searchers unknowingly penalize themselves, adding several unnecessary and unwanted months to their job-hunting campaign, by simply being ignorant of the best sources and methods for finding a job. The results can be disastrous and financially painful (particularly if unemployed).

Further compounding the difficulty is the fact that there is a plethora of misinformation out there about what works and what doesn't. It seems that just about everyone is an expert on the subject of job search. Just ask, and you'll get an earful of opinions on what to do and what not to do. Although well-intentioned, most of this misinformation is, unfortunately, given by persons who have had little or no real exposure to the job search process or the employment field in general.

It is my purpose here, as an employment professional with nearly 25 years experience, to draw your attention to the *facts* and away from the fiction. It is for this reason that I will be citing some solid statistical evidence for the recommendations I will be making.

The job-hunting strategy presented in this book is designed to intelligently address the two key barriers to effective and efficient job search. Clearly these two factors are the major stumbling blocks most responsible for derailing one's job search and are, more than any other factors, accountable for adding several unwanted months to the job-hunting cycle. These are:

1. Not knowing which employment sources to use (that is, which sources produce the best results).

2. Not knowing how to use these sources effectively.

Unfortunately, without proper training and guidance, most job seekers will approach the job search in a random, haphazard manner. Not knowing quite what to expect, they will begin by "sampling" various sources and techniques that they have heard about. Through a process of trial-and-error, sooner or later most stumble on a combination of things that begins to work. In the meantime, however, considerable valuable time has been lost and this trial-and-error process has taken a costly toll.

The purpose of this book is to help you to "jump start" your job search—to take the trial-and-error out of the job-hunting process—to replace it with proven sources and methods that work, right from day 1 of your job search.

IDENTIFYING THE "BEST" JOB SEARCH SOURCES

There are literally hundreds of sources that can be used to find jobs. The following is only a partial list of these:

advertising	employment agencies
search firms	computer job banks
state employment service	job fairs
alumni placement offices	networking
direct mail to employers	career consultants
employee referral programs	business consultants
banks	attorneys
professional associations	capital venture firms
trade associations	industry associations

Identifying and using the most productive sources, right from the beginning of your job search, can have far-reaching implications for both the success and length of your job search. Obviously, spending 100% of your time on 8 or 10 sources that produce only 2% of total job opportunities will have rather serious implications.

By contrast, selecting the right (most productive) employment sources from the very beginning of your search will have positive and immediate impact on the success and length of your job-hunting effort. Thus, for example, focusing most of your job-hunting efforts on the 3 most productive sources will surely translate into more job opportunities sooner. Knowing which of these sources are the most productive will undoubtedly give you a head start and ensure an early and successful conclusion to your job search.

So if you are going to successfully complete your job search in 60 days or less, it should be very clear by now that you will need to focus the lion's share of your attention on those sources that will produce the greatest results. Doing so will have significant impact on the length of your job search. To get off on the right track, however, you will need to know what these sources are.

Chapter 2 provides a clear answer to this question. It cites 3 separate employment studies that prove which of the various employment sources are the most effective. Interestingly, as you will discover in this chapter, only 3 employment sources account for some 92% of all jobs that are found. Knowing which 3 these are has profound implications concerning the length of your job search.

FULLY EXPLOITING THE *BEST* JOB SOURCES

Knowing which employment sources produce the best job results is simply not enough if you are committed to running a hard-hitting and effective job-hunting campaign. To fully capitalize on these sources, you must also know the most effective methods and techniques needed to do so.

Subsequent chapters of this book are devoted to instructing you in the use of various strategies and techniques that will allow you to fully exploit and utilize these key employment sources. These approaches are proven, tested methods known to be highly effective in achieving employment results. Each chapter dealing with these key job sources, therefore, provides both overall strategy and detailed, step-by-step instructions to enable you to capitalize on the use of them.

TIMING AND SEQUENCING

If you are committed to completing your job hunt in 60 days or less, the sequence and timing of job search activities are extremely important. In this regard, this book will not only provide you with the recipe (overall strategy) for *how* to conduct an effective job search, but will also instruct you regarding *when* to add the various ingredients as well.

You are provided with a carefully integrated, step-by-step approach to job hunting. Specific job search activities are not only well integrated, but also sequenced in such a way as to optimize the overall time required to conduct the job search. Put simply, you are told *what* to do, *how* to do it, and *when* to do it.

When major segments of the job-hunting strategy are carried out can have significant impact on the overall length of the job search. If you want to complete your search in 60 days or less, therefore, it is important that you pay particular attention to the specific timing recommendations provided throughout this book.

SUMMARY

The 60-day concept is one that will help you to plan and execute a highly effective job search strategy, which has been specifically designed to help you find the right job in 60 days or less. It will:

1. Help you to identify the *best* employment sources (those that statistically produce the most jobs).

2. Help you to eliminate *nonproductive* sources (so you don't waste time and effort).

3. Provide you with a systematic, step-by-step job search plan that will show you how to fully exploit the *best* (most productive) job sources.

4. Show you *when* to put certain elements of your job search in place, so that activities are running concurrently (allowing you to condense the length of your job search and get results sooner).

5. Instruct you in the use of various techniques that will
    allow you to shortcut conventional job search methods,
    saving considerable time.

    Utilizing the strategy and methods presented in this
book should allow you to conduct a highly effective job
search campaign and also provide you with the tools to cut
substantial time off of the job search process.

2

BEST SOURCES
FOR FINDING A JOB
What The Studies Show

B y far, the single biggest factor that can slow down a job search is wasting time with job sources that are known to produce little result. Thus, job searchers may waste as much as 80% to 90% of their time focusing on sources and techniques (direct mail campaign to employers, alumni placement offices, computer resume matching services, and so on) that statistically account for less than 5% of the jobs that are found.

This scenario is not an uncommon one, and can have a very significant effect on the time necessary to find employment. Such inefficiency can easily double, triple, or quadruple the length of your job hunt.

Before kicking off your job search, therefore, it is important to have a clear understanding of which job search sources and techniques are the most productive. By focusing your efforts on these particular sources, and ignoring nonproductive ones, you will identify many more job opportunities, and you will do so much sooner. This type of intelligent focus will be absolutely critical if your goal is to successfully complete your job search in 60 days or less. Without it, you can plan to spend several additional months looking.

It is for this reason that you need to be familiar with 3 important employment studies that clearly illustrate the importance of certain job sources in conducting a successful job search effort. These studies make it crystal clear that, despite the fact that there are numerous sources that can be used to find a job, there are only *3* basic sources that account for a very high percentage of all jobs found. In fact, as these studies will show, the same 3 sources account for between *89.5% and 93%* of all jobs found by jobs hunters. I like to refer to these 3 important job search sources as the "Big 3."

THE BEATTY STUDY

The first of these studies is a survey that I have personally just completed which, for simplicity's sake, I will refer to as the Beatty Study. The results of this study are provided on the pie chart shown in Figure 2.1. (Further details of this study are also presented in Chapter 6, "The Strong Case for Networking".) The data shown on this chart is the result of a survey conducted of 9 of the nation's largest outplacement consulting firms. Six of these firms provided "actual" data, while the remaining 3 provided "estimated" data.

If you are unfamiliar with the term "outplacement consulting," let me explain. Outplacement consulting firms are firms hired by companies, during large-scale employee downsizing efforts (or when letting go individual executives), to assist these displaced workers in organizing and conducting their job search. The assistance provided by these firms typically includes resume preparation and train-

THE BEATTY STUDY

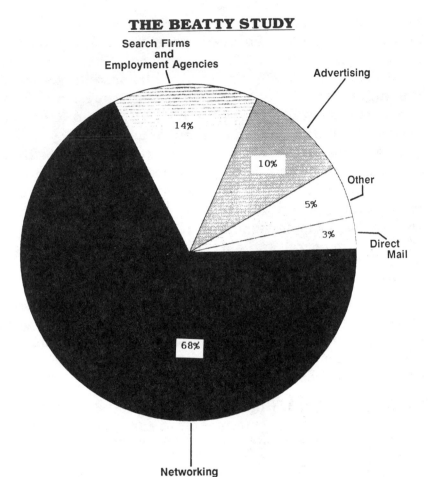

Figure 2.1 How jobs are found. A survey of major outplacement firms.

Source: Survey conducted of 9 major U.S. outplacement firms. Estimated database of over 10,000 persons.

ing in the various skills and techniques needed to conduct an effective job search (interviewing, job search planning, writing of cover letters, job offer negotiations, and so on).

Unlike the employment agency, these firms do *not* attempt to assist the employee in finding "specific" job opportunities. Instead, the focus of the professional outplacement consultant is to thoroughly train the employee in job search techniques and to act as a teacher, coach and counselor throughout the job search process. Today, outplacement consulting has become big business, with several of the larger major firms having annual revenues in the $10 to $75 million range, and providing job search training and assistance to over 2,000 client individuals a year.

As the Beatty Study shows, from the survey of these 9 major outplacement firms, some 68% of all jobs found by their clients were found through networking (personal contact), 14% through search firms and employment agencies, 10% through employment advertising, 3% through direct mail (to employers), and only 5% through all other sources combined.

The important message that comes through loud and clear from this study is that some *92% of all positions found* by these firms' clients came *from only 3 sources*—(1) networking (personal contact), (2) search firms and employment agencies, and (3) advertising. The specific percentage breakout for these 3 sources was as follows:

68%	Networking (Personal Contact)
14%	Employment Agencies/Search Firms
10%	Advertising
92%	Total (All 3 Sources)

The other important thing to realize about this study is the size of the database represented by the survey. Although the exact size of the study was not precisely determined at the time of the survey, due to the size of the 9 firms surveyed and the number of clients they handle each year, it is believed that this study reflects a volume of well over 10,000 job seekers. The data therefore represents the job hunting results of a sizable number of job seekers.

It is interesting to note, when reviewing the specific data reported by each of the firms surveyed (see detailed chart in Chapter 6), that there is quite a wide swing in the actual percentages of jobs found through use of each of the 3 employment sources. The following illustrates the degree of this variation:

Source	Low	High	Average
Networking	52%	92%	68%
Search Firms/Employ. Agencies	0.8%	21%	14%
Advertising	1%	22%	10%

Although it is believed that the "average" data for each of these 3 job sources, as shown on the pie chart, is fairly indicative of the general population of job seekers "as a whole" (both the Granovetter and U.S. Labor Department Studies presented later in this chapter appear to support this observation), it is felt that some of the extreme variation reported by the individual firms probably reflects the particular emphasis that the firm places on the use of a given job hunting source.

For example, during the course of the survey I was told by Jim Challenger of Challenger, Gray & Christmas (a Chicago-based outplacement consulting firm), that their firm places considerable emphasis on the use of networking as a principal job search methodology. This emphasis probably accounts for the fact that his firm reports 92% for networking.

Because of this emphasis, it could be argued that the data presented in the Beatty Study is misleading (since it may be influenced by the emphasis a firm elects to give to a particular job source). However, there are two additional studies which seem to support the results of the Beatty Study. These are the Granovetter Study and the U.S. Department of Labor Study. A comprehensive search of the literature, although identifying studies about what sources are used to "search" for jobs, does not reveal recent studies showing how jobs are actually "found." Unfortunately, the most recent studies on how jobs are found are the Granovetter and U.S. Department of Labor studies conducted in

1974 and 1975, respectively. Although both of these studies are clearly outdated, one cannot ignore the striking similarity between the findings of these studies and those of the study that I have recently completed. A comparison between the results of these studies strongly suggests that there has been little historical shift in the effectiveness of key job sources. What worked well then continues to work well today; the same 3 employment sources continue to be, by far, the dominant factors in finding employment.

Let's take a few minutes to examine both of these studies to see what they tell us about the effectiveness and importance of various employment sources to the job search process.

U.S. DEPARTMENT OF LABOR STUDY

While the focus of the Beatty Study was on professional, managerial and executive personnel, a separate study conducted in 1975 by the U.S. Labor Department covered both white collar and blue collar workers. (The results of this study are presented on the pie chart in Figure 2.2.)

The following summary presents the Labor Department's findings and also provides a comparison with findings of the Beatty Study as well:

	Labor Dept.	Beatty
Networking	63.4%	68%
Advertising	13.9%	10%
Search Firms/Employ. Agencies	12.2%	14%
Total	89.5%	92%

Since the Labor Department Study includes both blue and white collar workers, you would expect to see a slight shift in statistics when comparing the results of these two studies. Specifically, since blue collar workers rarely find jobs through employment agencies (and never through search

U.S. LABOR DEPARTMENT STUDY

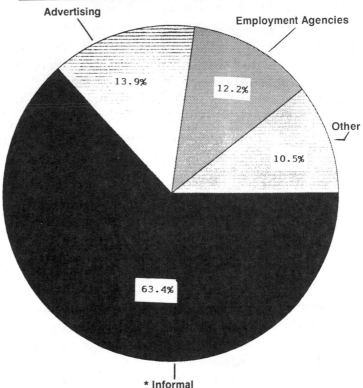

* Informal methods of job finding are those whereby the job seeker exercises their own initiative in building on personal contacts and making themselves known to potential employers.

Figure 2.2 U.S. Labor Department study of job-seeking methods used by American workers (blue collar and white collar).

Source: Job-seeking Methods Used by American Workers. U.S. Department of Labor, Bureau of Labor Statistics Bulletin #1886. 1975.

firms), you would expect to see slightly higher percentages for this category in the Beatty Study than in the Labor Department Study. This is the case, with the Beatty Study showing 14% for search firms and employment agencies, and the Labor Department reflecting a slightly lower 12.2%.

It is also believed that advertising plays a proportionately larger role in the recruitment of blue collar workers than in the recruitment of managerial and executive personnel. One would expect, therefore, to see the U.S. Department of Labor Study (which includes blue collar workers) attribute a higher level of results from recruitment advertising than the Beatty Study (which focuses on white collar workers only). This is also the case, with the Labor Department Study reporting 13.9% for advertising and the Beatty Study showing only 10%.

Most employment experts universally agree that the higher the level of the position, the greater is the role of search firms and networking (personal contacts) as job finding sources. This seems to be borne out in the Beatty Study (which includes white collar workers only), where a total of 82% of the positions found represented a combination of networking and search firms/employment agencies. In the Labor Department Study (which includes both white and blue collar workers), however, the number of positions found through this same combination of sources drops to 75.6%.

Despite some of these variations, which appear quite easily explained, the important message to be gleaned from both of these studies is that the same 3 sources (networking, search firms/employment agencies, and advertising) continue to account for a very high percentage of positions found. In this case, the Labor Department Study reports that a full 89.5% of all positions found (both white and blue collar) were found through the "Big 3." This compares to 92% for the Beatty Study (not a significant difference).

GRANOVETTER STUDY

Mark S. Granovetter, a Harvard sociologist, published an important labor study in the *Harvard University Press* in 1974, entitled "Getting a Job: A Study of Contacts and Careers." The findings of this study, as reflected on the pie chart shown in Figure 2.3, are not dissimilar from those found in the Beatty Study.

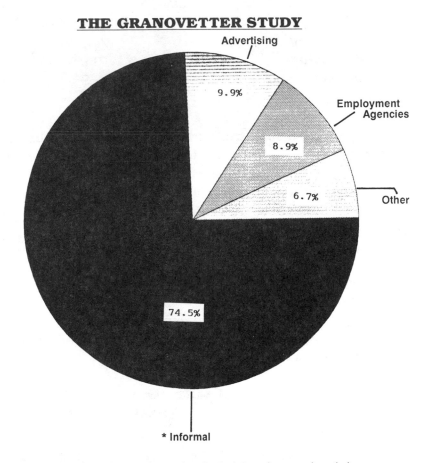

THE GRANOVETTER STUDY

Advertising

9.9%

Employment
Agencies

8.9%

6.7%   Other

74.5%

* Informal

* Informal methods of job finding are those whereby the job seeker exercises their own
initiative in building on personal contacts and making themselves known to potential
employers.

Figure 2.3 Granovetter study of how people get jobs (professional,
technical, managerial).

Source: Granovetter, *Getting A Job: A Study of Contacts and Careers,* Harvard University Press, Cambridge, 1974.

The Granovetter Study, as with the Beatty Study, targets professional, managerial and executive workers only, and does not include blue collar workers (as did the Labor Department Study). A comparison of both the Granovetter Study and the Beatty Study is shown on page 18.

	Granovetter	Beatty
Networking	74.5%	68%
Advertising	9.9%	10%
Search Firms/Employ. Agencies	8.9%	14%
Total	93.3%	92%

Here again, there is strong evidence to support the importance of the "Big 3" in the job search process. Granovetter's study shows that these 3 sources (networking, search firms/advertising agencies, and advertising) play a major role in finding jobs, with 93.3% of all jobs found through these sources compared to 92% in the Beatty Study.

COMBINED STUDY

Let's take a look at what the data tell us if we are to combine the results of these three studies into a single chart. The following is a summary of this combination.

	Beatty	Grano-vetter	Labor Dept.	Avg.
Networking	68%	74.5%	63.4%	68.6%
Search Firms/Agen.	14%	8.9%	12.2%	11.7%
Advertising	10%	9.9%	13.9%	11.3%
Total	92.%	93.3%	89.5%	91.6%

Combining the studies in this fashion clearly points to the fact that employment networking is by far the most productive source of jobs, accounting for an average of 68.6% of all jobs found. In fact, there were nearly *six times* the number of positions found through networking (personal contact) than the next most productive job hunting source.

Advertising and search firms/employment agencies appear to be equally productive as job search sources, accounting for a combined total of 23% of all positions found.

Thus, these two sources will be of great importance to the success of your job search, and will deserve some special focus when organizing and implementing your job search plan.

What has been left unsaid, is that *all other sources*, when combined, appear to account for a *puny 8.4%* of all jobs. This is a most significant statistic when considering how to best allocate your time in carrying out your job hunting campaign. Obviously, these sources should deserve little of your job search time if you are looking to shortcut the amount of time needed to successfully complete your job search.

THE KEY MESSAGE
FROM THESE STUDIES

If you are going to successfully complete your job search and find the right job in 60 days or less, then this chapter should serve as a "real beacon" for guiding your job search efforts.

Obviously, if only 3 sources (the "Big 3") account for some 92% of all jobs found, then the great bulk of your job search effort (and time) needs to be directed toward the effective use of these 3 sources. Why waste precious time and energy on a whole host of other random sources which, in combination, account for only 8% of all job search results? To do so will only waste precious time and add several weeks, if not months, to your job-hunting campaign.

Thus, the objective of this book is to focus your full attention on these few important sources, which we now know account for 92% of the jobs. By adopting a strategy which focuses full attention on these 3 sources, and by teaching you effective methods for exploiting and fully utilizing these sources, you will have at your fingertips a powerful job search strategy that will enable you to find the job you want and still cut considerable time from the job-hunting process. This job-hunting strategy will go a long way toward helping you to keep your job search to 60 days or less.

In order that we keep things in proper sequence and maximize use of your job search time, however, we will next need to address the subject of resume preparation.

3

RESUME POWER

Getting The Most
From Your
Employment Resume

I t is clear that the employment resume has a major role to play in the success of your job-hunting campaign. The success of your job search will require that you have a well-written, professional and effective resume as the anchor of your job search plan. Consider, for a moment, the key roles that this document must play.

First, the resume becomes the primary marketing document in your job search effort. It must do a sufficiently good job of setting forth your qualifications and credentials to convince a prospective employer that a personal interview is warranted.

Employment authorities concur that it is extremely rare that a company will agree to an employment interview without first having the opportunity to review a resume. If the resume is poorly written, there is little likelihood that an interview will result. Conversely, if well-written and providing convincing evidence of your ability to add value to the employer's organization, the prospective employer is likely to be persuaded that a face-to-face interview is in order. When using the resume as the cornerstone of your job search process, you must count on this important document to convey your background and capabilities to others in a concise, effective manner. A poorly organized resume will not accomplish this objective.

In addition to its obvious value as a marketing tool, the employment resume plays another key role as it relates to your job hunting program. It serves as a focal point during your employment interviews. In this sense, the employer uses this document as a kind of "roadmap" to guide discussions with you. If you have given a lot of care and thought to preparation of this document, the interviewer's attention will be focused on discussion of relevant skills and accomplishments, facilitating a smooth discussion that focuses on your strengths.

On the other hand, if the resume is disorganized and poorly prepared, the interview is likely to go a lot less smoothly, with the employer having to work much harder to understand your background and identify your major accomplishments. Since many with whom you will interview are not heavily experienced, skilled interviewers, you are leaving considerably more to chance. Lack of time or interview skills may cause the employer to conclude the interview discussions without having a solid understanding of your credentials for the position in question.

Another value of the resume that is frequently overlooked by the inexperienced job seeker is its "reference value." Your employment resume continues to serve as a reference document for the employer long after the interview is through. It is the key document that the employer will use to recall the specifics of your background and to compare your qualifications and credentials with those of others who are competing for a position. Clearly, a well-written resume can continue to sell your skills and capabilities following the job interview and will serve to enhance your competitive position as your credentials are compared and contrasted to those of other candidates.

Hopefully, I have provided sufficient reasons to convince you of the importance of your resume to the success of your overall job-hunting campaign. The rest of this chapter is committed to helping you to select and prepare a well-written, effective resume that will serve you well and enhance your marketability throughout the various phases of your job search campaign.

TYPES OF RESUMES

Although there are an almost endless array of resume types and styles to choose from, there are clearly only *two* resume formats that predominate the market and should serve as your model for resume preparation. These are the chronological resume and the functional resume. (A variation of the chronological resume, known as the "linear" resume, has also recently emerged as a highly popular resume format.) It is believed that chronological and functional resumes together represent approximately 80–90% of all resume formats used by the job seeker. A further breakdown suggests the following usage:

60–65%	Chronological Resume
20–25%	Functional Resume

Samples of these resume formats (including the linear resume) are contained at the end of this chapter for your reference.

SELECTING THE RIGHT RESUME

Selecting the right resume format for your use may not always be an easy decision, but is normally fairly straight forward. First, to simplify your decision, let me strongly recommend that you choose from either the chronological (including the linear) or the functional formats rather than some unconventional, "way out" style. Since these two formats predominate in the market, and are the formats with which employers are most familiar and comfortable, why buck conventional wisdom? Your personal job search is not the time to volunteer yourself for resume market research, but is rather the time for you to employ conventional methods that are time-tested and are known to work.

So, now we've gotten your choice down to one of two basic resume formats—the chronological or the functional. Now it's up to you to decide which one to use. To facilitate this choice, let's examine the characteristics, advantages and disadvantages of each.

THE CHRONOLOGICAL RESUME

Sample Resumes A, B, and C at the end of this chapter are examples of the chronological resume.

Characteristics

The chronological resume (including linear version) is by far the most popular and widely used resume format (60–65% of total resumes used). Review of the sample resumes at the end of this chapter will reveal that the focus of this style resume is on job progression. You will note that the Professional Experience section lists each position held in reverse chronological order—starting with the most recent position and working backward to the first professional job held. Because of the use of reverse chronology, this format is sometimes referred to as the "reverse chronological" resume.

Advantages

The key advantages of the chronological resume are as follow:

1. Since it is the most commonly used format, it is the resume style with which employers are most familiar and therefore feel most comfortable.

2. The logical, step-by-step listing of positions held makes this format both easy-to-read and easy-to-prepare.

3. This format allows the job seeker to emphasize career growth and progression (where he/she has experienced such)—two factors viewed favorably by most employers.

4. This format serves to highlight employment continuity (job stability) and career continuity—both seen as desirable attributes by employers.

5. This format serves to highlight the names of past employers, an advantage if these are well-known, prestigious companies.

Disadvantages

Key disadvantages of using the chronological format can include:

1. This format tends to emphasize or highlight certain obvious employment handicaps, including:

    a. Job hopping
    b. Employment gaps
    c. Underemployment
    d. Lack of career progress
    e. Little or no related experience
    f. Age

2. This format tends to draw attention to career progression, rather than to specific knowledge, skills or functional strengths.

3. This style resume tends to emphasize most recent positions where, in some cases, certain earlier experience may be more relevant to one's job search objective.

4. This format de-emphasizes certain key, job-relevant accomplishments where these occurred earlier in one's career.

THE FUNCTIONAL RESUME

See Sample Resumes D and E at the end of this chapter.

Characteristics

Unlike the chronological format, which focuses on job chronology, the functional resume format de-emphasizes positions held and draws the reader's attention to specific accomplishments by functional categories. Categories chosen are normally functional business areas (marketing, sales, market research, labor relations, employment, training, general accounting, cost accounting finance, and so on) that relate well to one's job search objective. Selected accomplishments and results are then delineated under each of these functional headings and the functional categories are listed in descending order on the resume, based upon their relative importance to the candidate's job search objective.

Advantages

1. The functional resume is the second most frequently used resume format (20–25%). Thus, it is a format with which most employers are familiar and feel relatively comfortable.

2. This format allows you to highlight specific functional accomplishments, skills, or capabilities even though these are more evident from positions held earlier in your career.

3. The functional format provides the opportunity to de-emphasize or hide certain undesirable information, such as:

    a. Lack of career progress
    b. Lack of career continuity
    c. Job hopping
    d. Lengthy or frequent unemployment
    e. Lack of required experience
    f. Lack of required education
    g. Age

4. Since it is not chronologically constrained, this format allows you the flexibility of listing your most apropos qualifications first, thus drawing maximum attention to them.

5. A functional format that is used to emphasize key skills and capabilities may sometimes suggest to the employer that there is more than one job where your capabilities could be utilized.

Disadvantages

1. Knowledgeable employment professionals are generally very suspicious of the functional resume, since this is the format frequently chosen by individuals who have something to hide, such as:

    a. Lack of career progress
    b. Lack of career continuity
    c. Frequent changes of job/employer
    d. Lengthy/frequent unemployment
    e. Recent period of underemployment
    f. Lack of required experience
    g. Lack of required education
    h. Age

    As a result, employment professionals often approach their review of the functional resume as if they are on a witch hunt—focusing on ferreting out "the problem" rather than on the candidate's qualifications for the position.

2. The lack of linkage between functions, accomplishments and specific employers causes frustration when the prospective employer attempts to make these connections as part of the preliminary evaluation process. The only recourse is to call the candidate for clarification. Most will not do this, and will simply move on to the next resume.

3. Key information like size, scope, and functional responsibilities of specific positions held with past employers is missing, again leaving the prospective employer guessing.

4. Generally, this format is more difficult to prepare than the chronological format, where there is a more logical continuity of thought.

THE FINAL CHOICE

From your review of the preceding advantages and disadvantages of both the chronological and functional resume formats, it should be pretty clear which of these formats best fits your particular needs. Wherever possible, however, I strongly recommend use of the chronological approach over the functional approach. This is particularly true when there has been good employment stability and career progression. Here are some additional guidelines, however, that should help you make the final choice between these two formats.

The functional resume should be used only when:

1. There is some major, negative information that, if highlighted, would serve to preclude further consideration of your employment candidacy. Such "knock-out factors" would include:

   a. Major career stagnation (no promotion or expansion of job responsibilities in the last six years)
   b. Obvious lack of career continuity (frequent, continuous changes in career direction)
   c. Frequent changes of jobs/employers (4 employers in 10 years, more than 7 employers during career, 3 or more recent jobs averaging less than 2 years duration, or 3 or more jobs during career that were less than 1 year duration)
   d. Lengthy or frequent periods of unemployment (unemployed for more than 1 year in last 10, 2 or more periods of unemployment exceeding 1 year, or 1 period of 2-year unemployment)
   e. Lack of critical experience considered essential to position
   f. Lack of required education (unless there is sufficient relevant experience to offset this requirement)

2. Critical skills and capabilities would not be sufficiently evident from use of the chronological format (where critical skills/capabilities were acquired from activities outside of professional career employment).

3. Recent employment history is unrelated (or distantly related) to current job search objective, and earlier career experience is clearly more relevant.

4. There has been a recent period of substantial under-employment (a significant reduction in job level, scope or responsibility) that has lasted for more than 1 year. (Note: Depending upon the magnitude and length of this underemployment, it may still be advisable to use the chronological format, simply providing a very brief description of this lesser position on the resume.)

5. Your career objective is not clearly defined and you wish to present your overall skills and capabilities so that the employer might consider your credentials more broadly in the light of various possible employment opportunities. (Note: This is a very ineffective way to conduct a job search and substantially reduces the probability of a successful outcome.)

IMPORTANCE OF RESUME APPEARANCE

In addition to selecting the resume format that serves your job search objectives, it is very important that your resume present a good appearance. From the employer's standpoint, your resume is an extension of you. If it is neat, crisp, and well-organized, it will create a very favorable impression—suggesting that you are someone who is careful and concerned about the quality of your work. Conversely, a sloppy, ill-conceived, disorganized resume will send quite a different message and may, in fact, ruin your chances of employment. It is critical to the success of your employment efforts, therefore, that you are attentive to the general appearance of your resume, and that you take the necessary steps to ensure that the appearance of your resume maximizes rather than detracts from your marketability.

The following are some basic guidelines to follow to improve the physical appearance and marketability of your resume:

1. Use a high quality bond paper in either white or buff.

2. Proofread and edit carefully to ensure proper spelling, grammar, punctuation, and comprehension. (If this is not your forte, seek help from a professional.)

3. Arrange to have your resume professionally typed. The professional image created is well worth the few dollars cost.

4. Avoid unique or unusual typefaces. Have your typist advise you on the proper style type to use.

5. Make effective use of highlighting (bold type) and underlining to facilitate ease of reading and appropriate topical emphasis. (Note the sample resumes at the end of this chapter for effective use of both, and tailor your resume accordingly.)

6. Avoid ragged or uneven margins.

7. Make sure that final copy is neat, well-spaced, uncluttered, and easy-to-read.

8. Final printing should be done by a professional printer using quality photo-offset printing equipment. Original copies printed on a quality laser jet printer are also quite acceptable.

SAMPLE RESUMES

The following resume samples are provided for your reference. Samples A, B, and C are examples of different variations of the chronological resume. The characteristic that they all have in common is that the emphasis is on positions held (job chronology). The Professional Experience section of the resume lists positions held in reverse chronological sequence, starting with the most recent and working back to the individual's first professional job.

Resume A is an example of the "classical" chronological resume, which uses a straight literary approach to describe job responsibilities and accomplishments. Resumes B and C, on the other hand, are examples of the "linear" chronological approach to resume writing. The linear approach presents certain of the job descriptive information (that is, job responsibilities and/or accomplishments) in a line-by-line linear format rather than in the narrative format utilized when preparing the "classical" chronological resume format.

Resume sample B is referred to as the "straight linear" approach, while C is an example of the "narrative linear" approach. The difference between the two is fairly obvious. In the straight linear approach, both job responsibilities and accomplishments are presented in line-by-line (linear) fashion. In the narrative linear format (see Resume Sample C), only job responsibilities are presented in narrative while accomplishments are presented in a linear (line-by-line) manner.

The linear chronological resume format has exploded in popularity in recent years and is rapidly becoming the resume style of choice by most job seekers and employment professionals as well. The advantages of linear over the classical chronological resume are as follow:

1. It is considerably easier to read.

2. It is easy to prepare.

3. The linear approach to describing job responsibilities and accomplishments tends to highlight these key factors.

Resume samples D and E are examples of the functional resume format. You will note that, although both resumes follow the functional format, Resume D chooses to emphasize specific business functions, while Resume E has elected to emphasize specific skills. This illustrates the difference between the functional-based and the skills-based functional resume.

Since it is not the purpose of this book to cover the subject of resume writing in detail, we will now move on to other subjects more directly relating to the subject of effective job search. Should you require detailed assistance in preparation of your resume, however, you may want to consider consulting my book on resume preparation, *The Resume Kit*, which should be available at your local library or bookstore. This will assist you by providing a detailed, step-by-step description of how to prepare a well-organized, effective and professional resume.

SAMPLE RESUME A
CHRONOLOGICAL(CLASSICAL)

DENISE K. MAC QUEEN
1325 Janson Way
Fullerton, CA 18225
Phone: (215) 557-0414 Home
(215) 557-3410 Office

OBJECTIVE: Senior level executive position with full responsibility for IMS function of major
company.

EXPERIENCE:

1982
to
Present

CORBOTT MANUFACTURING COMPANY, INC. (CORPORATE OFFICES)

Director of IMS (1990 to Present)
Report to Executive Vice President of Administration for this $2 billion, Fortune 200
manufacturer of pumps, valves, and fittings. Direct 110 employee department
and $8 million budget in the development, maintenance, and control of
corporate-wide computer information systems. Direct the activities of Corporate
Data Center and manage corporate-wide data communications network. Provide
systems development support to 4 divisions and 16 manufacturing facilities.

Developed and implemented first five-year corporate plan for systems
development and computer utilization. Successfully installed $7 million system for
computerization of sales forecasting, production scheduling, and materials control
functions estimated to save Company $6 million annually. Project completed
3 months early and 20% under budget.

Corporate Project Manager (1988-1990)

Managed activities of 8 to 12 project managers in design, installation, and start-up
of wide range of management information services projects. Annual budget of
$5 million.

Completed all projects on or before deadlines with 95% of projects finished under
budget. Major projects successfully completed include: Human Resource Data
Base, Payroll System, Order Entry System, Credit Control System, Production
Scheduling System, Finished Goods Inventory Control System, and Raw Materials
and Vital Supplies Control System.

Manager of Client Planning Services (1984-1988)

Managed department of 6 professionals responsible for planning the future
computer information needs of functional clients. Reviewed clients' strategic and
operating plans to determine management information needs necessary to meet
plan objectives. Identified required computer systems applications and developed
long-range information systems plans for 5 key functional areas: Industrial
Relations, Finance, Control, Manufacturing, and Procurement.

Denise K. MacQueen
Page Two

Senior Programmer Analyst (1982-1984)

Directed the activities of Analysts and Programmers in the development of numerous systems and programs covering a wide range of client information requirements.

1979
to
1982

MONTGOMERY CORPORATION (CORPORATE OFFICES)

Programmer Analyst

Developed numerous programs to meet the information requirements of a variety of clients.

EDUCATION: Ph.D., Cornell University, 1979
Major: Computer Science

M.S., Cornell University, 1977
Major: Computer Science
Data Resources Scholarship (2 years)

B.S., Lawrence University, 1975
Major: Mathematics   G.P.A. 3.5/4.0
Pennington Scholarship (4 years)

PERSONAL: Age 38
U.S. Citizen
Excellent Health

REFERENCES: Excellent references available upon request.

SAMPLE RESUME B
CHRONOLOGICAL (STRAIGHT LINEAR)

JOHN R. SMITH

119 South Maynard Road
Willingham, MA 94375
Telephone: (216) 552-8879

Accounting executive with over 14 years experience in increasingly responsible positions. Excellent reputation as creative, innovative and results-oriented senior manager who gets things done. Noted for applying computer systems in streamlining controllership operations. Full range of Accounting experience includes: capital and operating budgets, financial statements, accounting policies and procedures, auditing, taxes, general and cost accounting, accounts receivable, accounts payable and credit.

PROFESSIONAL EXPERIENCE:

1989
to
Present

SMITH DAVIDSON CORPORATION (CORPORATE OFFICES)

Assistant to Corporate Controller

* Report to Corporate Vice President of Finance for this $320 million manufacturer of computer hardware.

* Manage Corporate Accounting and Brickford Division Accounting functions (32 employees) including consolidation of financial statements for SEC and shareholder reporting.

* Reviewed and revamped accounting procedures and practices of Corporate Accounting Department (annual savings - $1.2 million).

* Directed computerization project to automate standard product cost build-up (annual labor savings - 500 hours).

* Organized, hired and trained Company's first Financial Planning Department.

* Initiated creative lease-back arrangement with foreign corporation on $52 million asset (annual savings - $1.6 million).

1986
to
1989

ZEBARD METAL CONTAINER CORPORATION (CORPORATE OFFICES)

Manager of Corporate Accounting (1987-1989)

* Reported to Chief Financial Officer of this $150 million manufacturer of overseas shipping containers.

* Managed staff of 14 professionals with responsibility for budget preparation/monitoring ($130 million), monthly and year-end closings, accounting system development/implementation.

John R. Smith   Page Two

* Computerized consolidation and analysis of monthly and year-end financial statements (annual savings - 800 manhours) and reduced closing turnaround time by 50%.

* Organized and managed task force which provided the first breakout of individualized division P&L statements.

* Raised capital to support $35 million capital expansion program at highly favorable rates and minimal affect on Company credit rating.

Senior Accountant (1986-1987)

* Reported to Manager of Corporate Accounting.

* Responsible for consolidation, review and analysis of Company's monthly and year-end closing statements.

1976
to
1986

BARLEY & JOHNSON, INC. (RICHMOND, VA)

Senior Accountant (1981-1986)

* Reported to Manager of Cost Accounting and Taxation of this public accounting firm.

* Provided cost and tax accounting consultation and services to clients in the $50 to $150 million range.

Accountant (1976-1981)

1972
to
1976

JORDAN ELECTRONICS, INC. (WOODBURY PLANT)

Senior Cost Accountant   (1974-1976)
Cost Accountant   (1972-1974)

EDUCATION

M.B.A., University of Northern Ohio, 1972
Major: Accounting/Finance
Bettinger Scholarship

B.A., Cannon College, 1970
Major: Accounting   G.P.A. 3.96/4.0
Magna Cum Laude

C.P.A., May 1973

SAMPLE RESUME C
CHRONOLOGICAL (NARRATIVE LINEAR)

DAVID R. JEFFRIES

36 Tartan Road, SW
Birmingham, AL 75663
Telephone: (314) 872-5533

Outstanding employment manager with over 5 years experience at the corporate and division level. Reputation for recruiting the hard-to-find. Thoroughly versed in all aspects of recruiting and employment with excellent track record of achieving results.

PROFESSIONAL EXPERIENCE

1978
to
Present

CONSTAR MANUFACTURING COMPANY, INC. (CORPORATE OFFICES)

Corporate Employment Manager, Operations (1983 to Present)
Report to Director of Corporate Employment of this $2.6 billion manufacturer of electrical products. Manage the staffing support for 25 plant operations function employing 13,000 employees. Support the hiring of 300 to 500 professional and managerial personnel annually at a cost of approximately $8 million.

* Successfully planned and managed the staffing of 3 new plant facilities employing 750 employees over 7 year period.

* Developed/implemented emergency staffing program to recruit 160 experienced engineers in 90 days to staff critical new capital program (all program goals met).

* Managed annual college recruiting program (37 campuses, 64 recruiting schedules) hiring an average of 220 professionals annually.

Employment Manager, Vanstar Division (1980-1983)
Reported to Division Director of Human Resources for this 2,500 employee division involved in the precision chemical coating of space vehicle parts. Focused on recruitment of hard-to-find Research Scientists specializing in the development of exotic chemical coatings for space travel applications.

* Developed creative approaches to identifying rare scientists including patent and computer literature searches.

* Reduced scientific recruitment backlog from 160 to 25 positions in three years.

* Trained over 100 scientists and technical managers in the use of advanced interviewing techniques.

Plant Personnel Manager, Millville Plant (1978-1980)
Reported to Plant Manager with responsibility to provide full range of human resource services to this chemical manufacturing plant of 600 employees.

* Successfully thwarted two union drives to maintain labor free manufacturing environment.

* Researched and directed implementation of experimental high performance work system using cutting edge sociotechnical approach.

* Installed new "Safety Alert" program, training all first iine supervisors and reducing lost-time injuries by 63%.

1974
to
1978

JOHNSON AND BARTON, INC. (WESTERLY PLANT)

Assistant Personnel Manager
Reported to Plant Personnel Manager of this 800 employee clothing manufacturing facility. Assisted manager in providing full range of personnel services to both salaried and hourly employees.

1970

BILTMORE ELECTRONICS, INC. (WESTERLY PLANT)

Personnel Assistant
Entry level personnel position in this 300 employee electronic equipment manufacturing plant. Handled wide range of projects and special studies in personnel field.

EDUCATION

B.A., University of Alabama, 1970
Major: Business Administration

PERSONAL

Age 35
Married, 2 Children
U.S. Citizen
Excellent Health

SAMPLE RESUME D
FUNCTIONAL (FUNCTIONS – BASED)

THOMAS MURPHY
132 Worrington Lane, SW
Dallas, TX 18253
Phone: (217) 767-5454 Home
(217) 877-0988 Office

<u>SUMMARY</u>: Results-oriented executive with over 14 years of demonstrated management leadership in all phases of marketing and sales in the chemical specialties industry. Known for innovative ideas that dramatically increase sales volume and business results.

<u>MAJOR ACCOMPLISHMENTS</u>:

<u>Marketing</u>:
- Established unique network of dealerships which catapulted Company to number 1 in European sales in specialty resins. (Export sales increased 75% to $225 million in 2 years.)
- Led national roll-out of new low viscosity resin product accounting for $150 million new sales in first year.
- Introduced 8 major new products accounting for increase in total sales of 40% ($210 million) in less than 4 years.
- Realized 225% increase in sales volume of old product in 2 years through market repositioning coupled with creative advertising.
- Led critical market research project supporting successful 20% increase in price of major product line with no loss in sales volume.

<u>Marketing & Sales Management</u>:
- Directed 185 employee marketing and sales organiza-tion for $400 million chemical specialties company.
- Managed marketing and sales organization of 128 employees for $525 million polyurethane manufac-ing firm.
- Served as Brand Manager for new resin product line ($15 million sales, 5 subordinates, $2 million budget).

<u>Sales</u>:
- Increased sales by 28% in one year while selling chemical specialties to pharmaceutical industry in 4 state area.
- Received national sales award for greatest sales volume increase in years 1977, 1980, and 1981.

WORK HISTORY:

1990 to Present	<u>Corrdigan Chemicals</u> (Corporate Offices) Director of Marketing
1982-1990	<u>Stanton Chemical Specialties, Inc.</u> (Corporate Offices) Director of Marketing and Sales (1986-1990) Marketing Brand Manager (1984-1986) Associate Brand Manager (1982-1984)
1977-1982	<u>Criswell Chemicals Corporation</u> (District Sales Office) Senior Sales Representative (1981-1982) Sales Representative (1977-1981)

EDUCATION: M.B.A., University of Chicago, 1977
Major: Marketing

B.S., Syracuse University, 1975
Major: Chemistry
President of Chemical Society

PERSONAL: Age 37
Married, 2 Children
U.S. Citizen
Excellent Health

REFERENCES: Excellent references available upon request.

SAMPLE RESUME E
FUNCTIONAL (SKILLS – BASED)

RICHARD HAVILAND
136 Westerly Lane
Detroit, MI 16335
Phone: (216) 757-4124 Home
(216) 557-3410 Office

SUMMARY: Over 15 years of dynamic, innovative R&D leadership in Fortune 500 companies. Demonstrated ability to achieve business goals through innovative technology. Broad range of technical expertise coupled with highly effective communications skills.

MAJOR ACCOMPLISHMENTS:

Managerial Leadership:
- Managed 500 employee corporate research center for Fortune 100 paper company ($32 million budget).
- Directed packaging & materials laboratory for leading fiber company (135 employees, $12 million budget).
- Managed 38 employee synthetic fiber research department ($1.2 million budget).

Technical Leadership:
- Realized $300 million annual savings through invention of unique forming device permitting 30% reduction in product raw material fiber.
- Spearheaded entry into $125 million new market through development of unique paper-like synthetic material.
- Increased sales by 15% in 2 years through development and introduction of 5 major new products for consumer market.
- Pioneered development of revolutionary new freezer wrap requiring less fiber and resulting in 25% cost reduction.

Innovation:
- Invented unique, highly successful magnetic forming device allowing high speed sheet formation of nonwoven materials.
- Pioneered new, innovative process permitting the formation of a synthetic fiber web on high speed wet lay technology paper machine.
- Developed thermal mechanical pulping process allowing 50% reduction in TMP energy requirements.

WORK HISTORY:

1990 to Present	Oregon Paper Company (Corporate Research Center) Vice President of Research and Development
1985 - 1990	Stratton Fiber, Inc. (Packaging and Materials Lab) Research Director, Packaging and Materials
1979 - 1985	Barton International Fiber, Inc. (Corporate Research) Research Manager, Synthetic Fibers (1983-1985) Senior Research Scientist, Polymers (1979-1983)
1977 - 1979	Velstar Electronics and Space Laboratory Research Scientist

EDUCATION: Ph.D., University of Michigan, 1977
Major: Chemical Engineering
Wilson Fellowship

M.S, Rochester Institute of Technology, 1975
Major: Materials Engineering   G.P.A. 3.67/4.0

B.S., Rochester Institute of Technology, 1973
Major: Chemical Engineering   G.P.A 3.8/4.0

PUBLICATIONS: 45 professional publications and papers

AFFILIATIONS: American Society of Chemical Engineers
American Chemical Society
Technical Association of Pulp & Paper Industry
American management Association

PERSONAL: U.S. Citizen
Excellent Health

REFERENCES: Excellent references available upon request.

4

DIRECT MAIL

How To "Jump Start" Your Job Search

I f you are looking to "jump start" your job search and be in the rather envious position of discussing specific job opportunities with employers within a matter of 3 or 4 weeks from the inception of your job search, one job-hunting technique I strongly recommend is use of a direct mail campaign targeted at executive search firms and/or employment agencies. Our experience has shown that, given the right circumstances, this can prove a highly effective method for "flushing out" some excellent career opportunities quickly. Clearly this direct mail approach should be a key weapon in your job search arsenal if you are planning to score a "direct hit" during the first 60 days (or less) of your job-hunting campaign.

You will recall from the statistics presented earlier in this book that direct mail was not known to be a very productive source of jobs. You may be wondering, therefore, why I am now strongly advocating the use of this approach as a vital job search method. The answer is simple.

The data presented earlier in this book represent statistics resulting from use of direct mail campaigns directed at employers. As a job-hunting source, such mail campaigns have, in fact, proven to be highly ineffective, and are felt to be barely worth the price of postage.

By contrast, however, what I am recommending is that your mail campaign be targeted at executive search firms and/or employment agencies—not employers. Search firms and employment agencies, as you may recall, are considered one of the "Big 3" employment sources and account for somewhere in the range of 10–15% of all positions found by the job seeker. There is some rather convincing evidence that a concerted effort, in the form of a mass mailing to these firms early in the job search, clearly has the potential to "up" these percentages considerably—not to mention shaving several months off of your job search as well.

Therefore, it is important that just as soon as your resume has been completed, the very next step in your job search should be to complete the research necessary to making this mailing. The next priority should then be to get this mailing to your local post office just as soon as possible. Do this right away, before you get bogged down in executing the other elements of your job-hunting campaign and lose precious time.

The beauty of this direct mail program as a job search technique is that it is something that can be done rather quickly at the very onset of your job-hunting campaign and, assuming you've got some reasonable credentials, can normally be expected to yield some fairly impressive results. An additional advantage is that by using this method at the start of your job search, the mailing will be out there quietly (or not so quietly) working for you while you are simultaneously pursuing other elements of your job search strategy. So, don't hesitate. Get it done now!

EXPECTED RESULTS

The results of a well-orchestrated direct mail campaign of this type can be relatively impressive. Our experience, as a consulting firm engaged in both executive search and outplacement consulting, has shown that direct mail will generally yield a response rate in the 2% to 5% range. Although results on the executive search side of our business have run a little closer to 5% , the response rate on the outplacement side (where direct mail has been used for job-hunting purposes) has typically been in the 2–3% range.

Thus, where the job seeker has some reasonable qualifications (and is not employed in a very narrow specialty or field where job opportunities are known to be unusually scarce), an 800-piece mailing to executive search firms has typically yielded somewhere between 18 and 24 positive inquiries. In fact, in our experience with such mailings, the normal response rate has actually exceeded 20 inquiries per mailing—meaning that our clients on average have had calls from better than 20 executive search firms to discuss specific job opportunities. And, importantly, most of these have come within 1 to 2 weeks of the date on which the mailing was made.

I am not aware of any other single job-hunting technique that can produce such dramatic results in so short a period of time. In fact one of our clients, who used this technique (a 900-piece mailing), within a period of 6 weeks from inception of his job search, had well over 20 search firm inquiries, received 3 job offers, and accepted a position that was an excellent match for his job search objective. This result was realized in 6 weeks, despite the fact that he took a week's vacation to attend a family reunion and was also known to leave our outplacement support center daily at about 2:30 P.M. to exercise at a local health club.

I want to be careful to point out that the direct mail campaign, although generally highly productive for those having

good employment credentials, may not always be the ultimate answer for every job seeker. It is very important, therefore, that you not rely solely on this technique as a means
to finding a job. There are other methods and approaches
described elsewhere in this book, depending on your employment qualifications, that could prove even more effective in your particular case. So, if you are serious about
finding a good position in 60 days or less, don't just plan
to use this mailing technique and then sit back and wait
for the calls to roll in. You are running against the clock
and need to get several other job-hunting activities going
simultaneously, if you are to launch a highly successful
employment campaign.

My purpose at this point, however, is to teach you
how to make an effective executive search firm/employment
agency mailing that will help get your job search off to a fast
start. I will leave discussion of other effective job-hunting
shortcut methods for other chapters of this book. So, let's
move on to discuss the steps you will need to follow in order to launch an effective direct mail campaign.

TARGETING THE RIGHT FIRMS

The first step in getting your direct mail campaign under
way is to decide what types of firms you will need to target
as the basis for your mailing. This is a key factor in ensuring the success of the direct mail approach. Essentially,
these target firms fall into 3 categories as follows:

1. Retained Executive Search Firm
2. Employment Agency (Contingency Firm)
3. Combination Retained & Contingency Firm

Which of these 3 categories you need to target will de-
pend upon the level and type of position you are seeking.

Since this is not always a "cut and dried" decision, however, it might be helpful at this point to help you understand the differences between these three types of firms. Being able to make this distinction should prove helpful in enabling you to make an intelligent and informed choice. Quite frankly, a poor choice of firms could well result in a considerable waste of postage and a rather disappointing result. It is important, therefore, that you have a clear understanding of the differences between these firms, and that your choice be made wisely.

DISTINGUISHING SEARCH FIRMS FROM EMPLOYMENT AGENCIES

Today, there appears to be much confusion among the general public about the difference between an "executive search firm" and an "employment agency." Unfortunately, employment agencies have found it advantageous in recent years to further blur this important distinction, by referring to themselves as "executive search firms" or "executive search consultants." The use of these labels by the employment agencies is quite misleading, however, and serves to seriously confuse the issue in the minds of both the job seeker and employer alike. If you are to make a proper choice between these two types of firms for purposes of your mail campaign, however, it is extremely important that you understand the subtle distinctions.

To attempt to lend some clarity to this discussion and eliminate the confusion that now exists on this subject, I have elected to use the term "retained" executive search firm. This is intended to contrast these firms with the "contingency" employment agencies. The significance of the word "retained" versus "contingency" gets at the very heart of the distinction between these two types of firms. These two terms relate to the manner in which these firms receive payment for their services.

For purposes of clarity, I define the "retained" executive search firm as a true management consulting firm that is retained (under a written contract) by the employer to represent them (on an exclusive basis), for the purpose of recruiting a key manager or senior executive. These firms, like all true consulting firms, are paid a "retainer fee" for their consulting time by the firm that has retained them to carry out the search assignment.

The important thing to realize is that the true executive search consultant is paid by the employer for his or her consulting time, without regard to the final outcome of the search assignment. Put differently, payment of the executive search consulting fee is made for the consultant's time and is not "contingent" upon actual placement of a finalist candidate in the position they have been retained to fill.

Thus, it is common practice in the executive search profession for the consultant to bill out the full retainer fee (usually amounting to 30–35% of the total annual income of the position to be filled) in 3 equal installments over the first 3 months of the search assignment. Additionally, in accordance with their contract with the client, the executive search firm will normally invoice the client company for all expenses associated with carrying out the search assignment (telephone, travel to interview finalist candidates, postage, and so on).

Obviously, a true executive search consulting firm must be highly experienced and professional in order to command payment of retainer fees, with no guarantee of results to the client who has hired them. It is not uncommon for their fees to be $30,000 or higher for a given search assignment. Thus, for the most part, these firms tend to be staffed with highly experienced and seasoned professionals, who have long earned a reputation for excellent, consistent results in finding exceptional management talent for the clients whom they serve. By virtue of their excellent reputations, the better executive search consulting firms' services are in demand, and they are repeatedly chosen by client companies to assist in filling the higher level managerial and executive positions in the client's organization.

Most retained executive search firms have a "cutoff" below which they will not undertake an assignment. Based upon 1990 dollars, many of these firms will not consider an assignment for positions paying annual salaries of less than $60,000 or $70,000. Some of the major "blue chip" search firms, in fact, will not consider assignments for positions paying less then $125,000 per year minimum. (Increase these cutoff salary levels by 5% per year, since 1990, to arrive at today's equivalent.)

It should be obvious from these compensation cutoff levels that the focus of retained executive search firms is on filling higher level management and executive positions. Generally, the focus of these firms is on upper middle management level positions and above. It is rare that these will agree to undertake assignments to fill lower middle management, first line supervisory, or professional level positions.

By contrast, the employment agency or "contingency" firm does not have sufficient experience and reputation to warrant payment of a retainer fee by the client whom they serve. Instead, such firms are paid on a "contingent" basis. This means that they are paid *only* if and when they have been successful in filling the position, and not before.

Technically, the employment agency is the agent of the employment candidate, and not the employer. Such firms are not normally under contract with the employer, and have not been granted exclusive rights as the sole source in filling the position. They are thus in competition with other employment sources (other employment agencies, recruitment advertising, employee referrals, and so on) in filling the position, and must take their chances on getting paid.

Although employment agencies clearly have an important role to play in the employment market, and some are quite good at what they do, these firms are seldom chosen by client companies to fill higher level management and executive positions. For the most part, therefore, these "contingency" firms focus on filling lower level managerial, supervisory, and professional level positions. Some may also handle administrative support positions (clerks, secretaries, administrative assistants, technicians, and so on).

HYBRID FIRMS

Now that I've worked so hard to help you distinguish the difference between the executive search firm and the employment agency, I'm going to muddy the waters by telling you about "hybrid" firms. These firms are a cross between the executive search firm and the employment agency.

Generally, the hybrid firm has built sufficient rapport with certain of their clients to warrant the payment of either a full or partial retainer fee. With these clients the firm has usually also been able to secure a contract granting them exclusivity in filling the position for which they have been retained. With other clients, however, they have not yet reached this level of relationship and continue to work on a contingent, nonexclusive basis as an employment agency.

As you might suspect, the hybrid firm normally operates at a level somewhere between the executive search firm and the employment agency, focusing mainly on the filling of middle management and senior level professional positions. Occasionally, these firms may handle a senior level management or executive position. Likewise, they may also occasionally handle assignments at the first line supervisory or professional level. It is rare, however, that the hybrid firm would be engaged in recruiting for administrative support positions (clerks, secretaries, administrative assistants, technicians, and so on).

SELECTION GUIDELINES

The following guidelines are provided to assist you in selecting the right type(s) of firms as the basis for your direct mail campaign:

Executive Search Firms

Choose retained executive search firms as your "primary" target if you are seeking a position at the upper middle management or executive level. Choose this category, as a "secondary" (supplemental) target if you are looking for a middle management level or senior professional position. Do *not* select this category if you are seeking a first line supervisory, professional, or administrative support level position.

Hybrid Firms

Select hybrid firms as a "secondary" (supplemental) source for your mailing if you are seeking an upper middle management or executive level position. Choose this as your "primary" category if your job search objective is a middle management or senior professional level position. Pick this as a "secondary" (supplemental) category if you are looking for a position at the first line supervisory or junior professional level. Do *not* select hybrid firms if you are looking for an administrative support type position.

Employment Agencies

Choose employment agencies as a "primary" target group for your mail campaign if you are seeking a first line supervisory or junior level professional position. This category should also be a "primary" choice for persons looking for a nonexempt administrative support position, provided there is advance knowledge that the agency accepts assignments at this level (many do not). Additionally, employment agencies should be selected as a "secondary" (supplemental) target category for those seeking positions at the middle management or senior professional level. Generally, these firms should *not* be chosen by persons seeking senior middle management and executive level positions (except as a last resort, in the event that prior mailings targeted at executive search firms and hybrid firms have not produced expected results).

Having made the selection of the type firm(s) most appropriate to the level of position you are seeking, your next step is to secure the directories necessary to preparing your mailing list.

HOW TO DEVELOP THE MAILING LIST

I have done some research to help you to acquire the names of those firms who publish directories that list executive search firms, hybrid firms, and employment agencies. A summary of these firms and their publications is provided below for your convenience.

So that you do not unnecessarily delay your job search I would suggest that, on the first day of your search, you call and order these directories on an immediate basis. Many of the publishers will accept credit cards as the basis for payment rather than requiring a personal check. By providing them with your credit card number and placing your order by phone, these directories can frequently be sent out on the same day.

To further expedite your receipt of these directories, you may want to arrange prepayment with Federal Express so that the directory can be sent to you overnight. By providing the publisher with your Federal Express number, therefore, they can immediately ship the directory to your attention for next day delivery. Another option is to authorize the publisher to charge your credit card for the cost of the Federal Express charge and arrange for immediate shipment for delivery to you on the following day.

The point is, with a little forethought and creativity, a lot of time can be saved in getting this material to you. This time savings can be extremely important if you are serious about wishing to successfully conclude your job search within a 60-day timeframe.

MAILING LIST SOURCES

The following is a summary of mailing list directories published by different firms for your use in preparing your direct mail campaign. Although there are likely other publishers who publish similar directories, these are the ones with which I am most familiar. Phone numbers have been included in the summary so that you can expedite shipment of the directories and save valuable job search time.

The prices of these directories seem to be escalating quite a bit in recent years. The prices shown here are those being charged by these firms as of the date of publication of this book. Due to this trend of rapid escalation, however, you may wish to verify the prices of these directories at the time you place your order. In this way, you may avoid the possibility of an unpleasant surprise.

1. National Association of Personnel Consultants
   1432 Duke Street
   Alexandria, VA 22314
   Phone: (703) 684-0180
   Publication Name: *ACCESS*
   Description:

A directory listing some 2,200 private employment agencies who are members of the National Association of Personnel Consultants. Includes name of agency, address, phone number, and name of contact. Information is presented 3 ways: (1) alphabetical, (2) geographically, and (3) by employment specialty.
Approximate Price: $21.95

2. Kennedy & Kennedy, Inc.
    Templeton Road
    Fitzwilliam, NH 03447
    Phone: (603) 585-6544
    Publication Name: *Directory of Executive Recruiters* (Personal Edition)
    Description:
    Directory contains over 3,700 main and branch office locations of both retained executive search firms and employment agencies (contingency firms). Importantly, there is a breakout of these two types of firms, with the contingency firms listed in a separate section. Firms are listed alphabetically including name, address, key contacts, and the directory includes a brief description of firm's speciality as well as minimum salary cutoff. Indexes include breakout by geography, industry, and management function specialization.
    Approximate Price: $39.95

3. Association of Executive Search Consultants
    17 Sherwood Pl.
    Greenwich, CT 06830
    Phone: (203) 661-6606
    Publication Name: *AESC Membership Directory*
    Description:
    Directory lists the 102 member firms in alphabetical order (including all branch offices). Includes firm's name, address, and phone number for both the corporate and branch offices. Members are retained executive search firms only (no contingency firms) and focus on filling management and executive positions paying annual salaries over $60,000. Several have overseas offices, which are listed.
    (*Note:* These firms are considered the "blue chip" firms in the executive search industry.)
    Approximate Price: $25.00

4. American Business Directories, Inc.
    Division of American Business Lists, Inc.
    5707 S. 86th Circle
    Omaha, NE 68127
    Phone: (402) 593-4600
    Publication Name: *Executive Search Consultants*
    Description:
    Listing of 6,294 executive search consultants published
    monthly from the "Yellow Pages" of the telephone directory.
    Information is presented geographically and includes firm's
    name, address, and phone number (including area code).
    (*Note:* The fact that a firm elects to list itself as an "executive
    search consultant" for purposes of advertising in the "Yellow
    Pages" is no guarantee that the firm is a "retained" versus a
    "contingency" firm.)
    Approximate Price: $200

5. American Business Directories
    Division of American Business Lists, Inc.
    5707 S. 86th Circle
    Omaha, NE 68127
    Phone: (402) 593-4600
    Publication Name:
    Employment Agencies Directory—Eastern Edition
    Employment Agencies Directory—Western Edition
    Description:
    Arranged geographically, this directory lists 11,400 employ-
    ment agencies (Eastern Edition) and 6,062 employment agen-
    cies (Western Edition) including firm's name, address, and
    telephone number (including area code). Information is ob-
    tained monthly on-line from the "Yellow Pages" of the
    telephone directory, and can be broken out by state and
    city.
    Approximate Price:
    Eastern Edition $375
    Western Edition $220

6. Bob Adams, Inc.
    840 Summer Street
    Boston, MA 02127
    Phone: (617) 767-8100
    Publication Name: *Job Bank Guide to Employment Services*

Description:

Guide contains over 4,000 employment agencies, executive search firms, temporary help services, and career counseling centers including organization's name, address, and telephone number. Includes geographical and specialization indexes.

(*Note:* Directory was out-of-print as of this writing, but copies may be available at your local library. Firm is considering an additional printing of this publication.)

Approximate Price: $129.95

7. American Management Association
   135 West 50th Street
   New York, NY 10020
   Phone: (212) 903-7912
   Publication Name: *Executive Employment Guide*
   Description:
   Guide contains over 100 executive search firms, employment agencies, job registers and job counselors. Information is arranged alphabetically by name of firm and includes address, phone number and type of firm.
   Approximate Price:
   Free to A.M.A. members
   $10 to nonmembers

SIZE AND COMPONENTS OF MAILING

The size of your mailing is entirely up to you. Generally, I recommend at least a 500-piece mailing, with a personal preference for something in the 800- to 900-piece range.

Obviously, with an expected positive return of 2–3% , the larger the mailing, the larger will be the response—and the greater will be the number of job opportunities you may have the chance to consider. Cost, however, may be a factor here since the cost of the U.S. postage stamp keeps going up and mailings of this type are no longer an inexpensive proposition.

The components of your direct mail campaign are quite simple. They consist of a basic cover letter and a copy of your employment resume. The cover letter should be no more than a single page in length, and should include the following basic elements:

1. Introductory Paragraph (Objective Statement)

    • Statement of job search objective
    • Reference to firm's clients

2. Second Paragraph (Background Summary)

    • Qualifications summary
    • Education
    • Relevant Experience

3. Third Paragraph (Selling Yourself)

    • Value Statement
    • Key contributions (quantitative statements, where possible)
    • Specialized knowledge
    • Unique skills and capabilities
    • How you can add value to the client organization

4. Fourth Paragraph (How to reach you)

    • Phone numbers
    • Times to reach you

5. Final Paragraph (Close)

    • Statement of appreciation

The cover letter at the end of this chapter is provided as a model so that you might use it as a guideline for constructing one of your own. You will notice how this sample letter incorporates the recommended components in the outline just presented. This particular cover letter approach has been used quite successfully by clients who have been through our outplacement (job search training) process. Results have been consistently quite good, so I am recommending this or similar letter format to you for use in your own direct mail campaign.

I have now provided you with all of the ingredients necessary to formulate and execute a highly effective direct mail campaign. Clearly, this direct mail campaign needs to be an important building block in your overall job search program if you are going to be successful in finding your desired job opportunity within the 60-day target objective.

SAMPLE COVER LETTER (DIRECT MAIL CAMPAIGN)

425 East Lemon Street
Orchard Hills, NY 77312
March 26, 1993

Mr. Stephen Baker
Senior Vice President
Baker, Lees and Fulton, Inc.
Suite 255
Society Towers
300 Commerce Square, East
Chicago, IL 47389

Dear Mr. Baker:

I am seeking a senior level position in Operations management. Perhaps one of your current or future clients may have an interest in my capabilities.

I hold an M.S. degree in Industrial Management from the University of Michigan and have over 15 years experience in Operations, with 6 years in management. As Director of Manufacturing for Fluidyne Corporation, a $200 million manufacturer of specialty pumps for the chemical industry, I manage a staff of 32 professionals and direct all manufacturing operations for 4 manufacturing sites, employing over 3,000 employees.

In the past two years, I am credited with delivering annual savings of nearly $6 million as the result of several innovative programs. These have included statistical process control, Just-In-Time management, product stream management, and socio-technical systems. I pride myself on staying current with all major new developments in the field of Operations, and am quick to apply new techniques which show promise for improving bottom line results.

If one of your clients seeks a highly motivated Operations executive who has a demonstrated record of substantial cost reduction and productivity improvement, perhaps you will think of me.

Should you wish to contact me during the day, I can be reached at (275) 492-0785 on a confidential basis. Thank you for your consideration.

Sincerely,

David P. Cortlund

Enclosure
DPC/ret

5

TAPPING THE
FULL POWER
OF RECRUITMENT
ADVERTISING

I f you are truly serious about successfully completing your job search in 60 days, you will need to approach recruitment advertising a lot differently than the typical job seeker. Simply reading the employment want ads in one or two of your local newspapers is not going to do it! Instead, there is a specific strategy that you will need to apply to recruitment advertising that will allow you to maximize the effectiveness of this job source and provide you with the potential to take weeks, if not months, off your job search effort. This chapter will show you how to effectively use this strategy to your advantage.

As we already know from statistics presented earlier in this book, advertising is one of the top three most productive job-hunting sources. Generally, it is believed to account for 8–10% (some sources estimate as high as 15%) of all jobs found by job seekers. Along with employment networking (finding jobs through personal contact) and executive search firms/employment agencies, it accounts for an estimated 92% of all positions filled—falling just slightly behind search firms/employment agencies in its overall importance to the job search process. We might thus think of employment advertising as one of the "Big 3" of job search sources.

WHEN TO READ RECRUITMENT ADVERTISING

Many job-hunters unwisely use the daytime and early evening hours to read and respond to employment advertisement. This is time that could be far more effectively utilized for employment networking purposes, and should not be used for reviewing and responding to advertising.

Since employment networking (which is known to account for 70–80% of all jobs found by job seekers) can normally only be done during the day or early evening hours, if you are serious about finding a job quickly you will want to avoid advertising-related activities during these critical hours. Instead, reading and responding to employment advertisements are best left for the later evening hours and weekends, when carrying out employment networking activities is not a practical consideration.

So, if you are committed to running a highly efficient job-hunting campaign and cutting considerable time off of the job search process, confine the reading of employment advertising to evening hours and weekends. Don't waste valuable networking time for this purpose.

ADVERTISING SATURATION STRATEGY

Often the typical job seeker takes a rather haphazard, random approach to the use of recruitment advertising as a job-hunting source. Typically, his or her efforts are limited to picking up the Sunday edition of one or two key news-papers. Perhaps, as an afterthought, he or she might also occasionally thumb through a trade association newsletter or professional journal in search of appropriate employer want ads.

This rather limited and haphazard approach is clearly not an effective way to maximize the power of employment advertising as a "Big 3" job search source. Nor will it do much to shorten the length of your job-hunting campaign. Instead, if you are to realize the full potential of recruit-ment advertising as a key job-hunting source and simulta-neously reduce the time necessary to finding a good job, a much more strategic approach to recruitment advertising is definitely called for.

In order to tap the full power of employment advertising as a job seeker, from a strategic perspective you will need to target 4 distinct segments of the job market to achieve meaningful coverage and good market penetration. These market segments are:

1. The National Market

2. Your Target Geography

3. Your Target Industry(s)

4. Your Professional Specialty

Think of this strategy as a kind of "saturation bombing." If you systematically target, collect and review all employ-ment advertising from these 4 principal target markets, it is highly unlikely that you will miss your target (employer ad-vertisements of interesting positions). The more your strat-egy permits you to blanket these 4 market segments, the higher is the probability you will get a "direct hit"—and the sooner you will find meaningful employment.

This broader, systematic approach to the use of em-ployment advertising is a far more comprehensive strategy than that employed by most job hunters. It simply doesn't leave much to chance, and serves to substantially improve the probability that you will become aware of key advertised positions within the geography that you have chosen as your "preferred" target area.

Although this approach can at first appear to be somewhat costly in the short term because of the high cost of publication subscriptions, in the longer term it can prove highly cost-effective by helping you to drop months off of what otherwise might have been a rather protracted job search. Besides, with a little resourcefulness, even the short-term costs can be reduced substantially through the effective use of the resources offered by your public or company library.

Let's now take a closer look at how to effectively implement this advertising saturation strategy.

THE NATIONAL MARKET

There are several large "national" newspapers that you may want to consider for use in your job search. By "national," I mean that these papers have fairly extensive circulation beyond the cities in which they are published. Because of their mass circulation, these newspapers are particularly popular with employers as preferred media for employment advertising, since their large circulation often translates into good advertising response (that is, lots of resumes). Additionally, due to the large circulation of these papers beyond the immediate cities in which they are published, many of these papers (particularly the Sunday editions) are known to provide excellent regional coverage and are therefore used by employers who wish to target their recruitment advertising to certain regions of the country (for example, the *Atlanta Journal* is often used to target the Southeastern United States and the *Boston Globe* to target the New England market).

The names of these major national papers, along with the telephone numbers of their subscription departments, are provided here for your convenience.

Boston Globe	1-800-225-9962
The Wall Street Journal	1-800-237-7100
New York Times	1-800-631-2580
Philadelphia Inquirer	(215) 665-1089
Baltimore Sun	(301) 539-1280
Washington Post	1-800-424-9203
Atlanta Journal	(404) 522-4141
Cleveland Plain Dealer	(216) 344-4080
Chicago Tribune	1-800-972-9515
Houston Chronicle	1-800-735-3800
Dallas Times Herald	(214) 720-6111
Los Angeles Times	1-800-528-4637
San Francisco Chronicle	(415) 777-1111
Seattle Times	(206) 464-2111
Denver Post	(303) 820-1010

With the exception of *The Wall Street Journal*, you will want to order the Sunday edition of these papers, since it is the Sunday edition which contains the lion's share of the recruitment classified ads. *The Wall Street Journal*, on the other hand, runs the bulk of its employment advertising on Tuesdays and Fridays.

Should the cost of these subscriptions be a concern, you may want to check the periodicals or reference section of your local library. Libraries frequently carry the Sunday editions of these major newspapers. This approach could result in considerable savings, since many of these papers require minimum subscription terms and are not cheap.

It is important not to base your decision to include or exclude one or more of these major newspapers from your target group simply on the basis of the location published. This could be a mistake.

Since many national companies utilize these major publications to secure good "regional" advertising coverage, the location of a given newspaper can often have little to do with the location of the actual position being advertised by a firm. Thus, a company located on the West Coast may well use the *Chicago Tribune* to target the Midwest market, even though the position advertised is located in Portland, Oregon. Likewise, a Boston-based company seeking to recruit persons from the Midwest for positions located in New Hampshire, may also elect to use the *Chicago Tribune*. So, picking one of these newspapers on the basis of its location alone may prove somewhat misleading.

Another factor to keep in mind, when deciding which of these national newspapers to select, is the "geographical saturation" of specific industries. For example, it is known that the Philadelphia area has an unusually large population of pharmaceutical companies. Thus, many Midwestern pharmaceutical companies advertise in the *Philadelphia Inquirer* in an effort to attract talent from the Philadelphia area, even though the positions they advertise are located in the Midwest. Thus, if pharmaceutical is one of your target industries, you will likely want to subscribe to the *Philadelphia Inquirer*, even though you may wish to live in areas of the country other than the East Coast. So "geographic saturation" of your target industry(s) should play a key role when deciding which of these national newspapers to select. Select those papers published in the cities known to have a high population of firms from your target industry(s).

When selecting major newspapers as part of your national employment advertising coverage strategy, there are two additional publications that warrant your serious consideration. These are *The National Ad Search* and the *National Business Employment Weekly*. Both newspapers are solely dedicated to employment advertising, and both are national in scope. A brief description of each of these publications, including free 800 subscription telephone number, is provided for your convenience.

The National Ad Search. This is a tabloid that weekly reprints some 2,000+ employment want ads from 72 major U.S. newspapers. These recruitment ads are arranged into 55 executive, managerial, and technical categories for easy reference. You can subscribe to this tabloid by calling 1-800-992-2832 toll-free.

National Business Employment Weekly. This weekly tabloid is available at many newsstands and drugstores, and is a consolidation of all the past week's recruitment advertising from the 4 regional editions of *The Wall Street Journal.* It can be ordered by calling 1-800-562-4868 toll-free.

YOUR TARGET GEOGRAPHY

Now that you have selected those major, national newspapers and weekly tabloids necessary to assure you of adequate coverage of the national employment advertising market, you will next need to focus your attention on that segment of the market that comprises your preferred geography (your geographical target). The process for accomplishing this is fairly simple.

In many (if not most) cases you will already have chosen one or more of the major, national newspapers offering good regional coverage of your geographical target. You will now need to supplement these publications by also subscribing to the Sunday editions of smaller city newspapers located within the geographical areas you have targeted for your job search.

To achieve this target first simply use a map to pinpoint key metropolitan areas within your geographical target area. Then, using your telephone directory "Yellow Pages," contact a local advertising agency and request their assistance in helping you to identify the names and telephone numbers of the major newspapers published in each of these target cities. This information is readily available, and is generally at the advertising agency's fingertips. A quick call to the subscription department of these newspapers should have their Sunday edition on your doorsteps in a matter of a few short days.

Between these smaller city publications and the major national newspapers, which provide good regional coverage, you will have employed a fairly comprehensive strategy for assuring coverage of your targeted geographical area from the recruitment advertising perspective. Now, your next step is to put in place a strategy to cover those specialty publications which carry employment advertising aimed at your target industry(s).

YOUR TARGET INDUSTRY(S)

In order to ensure that you are getting full mileage from employment advertising as a key job-hunting source, you will want to be sure that your publication subscriptions include those specialty publications containing recruitment advertising that is specifically aimed at your target industry(s). Such highly targeted employment advertising is frequently found in industry association published journals and newsletters. In some cases, however, such journals and newsletters are published by private organizations, but are targeted at specific industry segments.

If you are uncertain how to go about identifying such specialty publications, let me suggest the following method:

1. Using the *Encyclopedia of Associations* (frequently found in public and company libraries), identify those industry or trade associations specific to your target industry(s).

2. Using the phone numbers provided in this encyclopedia, contact the key officers of these association(s)

and ask their advice concerning those industry specific newsletters and journals most frequently chosen
by member employers for recruitment advertising purposes.

3. Find out from the association officers how to go about
    ordering a subscription to these publications, and order
    your subscription accordingly.

As an alternative to ordering and paying for subscriptions to these key specialty publications (some can be
rather expensive), you may want to check the business periodicals section of your local library. If not available at your
public library, then see if you can arrange to access the library of an industry member company located near you. Often times such firms will carry these publications, and they
may be quite willing to allow you access to their library for
a few hours each month, if you ask nicely.

By obtaining these specialty journals and newsletters,
you will have now put in place an excellent strategy for
systematically keeping abreast of job opportunities that develop in your target industry(s). These kind of publications
have long been used by employers as highly effective media
for targeting their employment advertising toward specific
industry segments.

YOUR PROFESSIONAL SPECIALTY

Having put in place the overall job search strategy that
will allow you to effectively monitor recruitment advertising
from the national, geographical, and industry perspective,
you now need to incorporate a strategy for systematically
monitoring employment advertising aimed at your particular professional specialty (accounting, finance, engineering,
manufacturing, human resources, or whatever).

The process for identifying key specialty publications that are aimed at your target profession is not dissimilar from that used in putting in place the target industry(s) segment of your advertising strategy. This process is as follows:

1. Using the *Encyclopedia of Associations*, identify those professional societies and associations that are organized for the benefit of your targeted professional specialty.

2. Using the phone numbers provided in this encyclopedia, contact the officers of these organizations and ask their advice concerning those publications (journals, newsletters, and so on) most frequently used by employers to target association members for employment purposes.

3. Find out from association officers how to go about subscribing to these publications.

Since subscription to some of these publications can sometimes be expensive, you may want to secure the names and contact information for a couple of association members who live in your area. Many members may be quite willing pass their copies of these publications along to you once they are finished with them. Perhaps they may also still have some recent issues lying around that they might provide to you.

ALTERNATE WAYS TO USE PUBLICATIONS

Although the primary purpose for subscribing to the various publications described in this chapter is to monitor and respond to relevant employment advertising, effective use of these publications dictates that you also pay close attention to other factors that could provide excellent employment leads. These include:

1. Company expansions

2. Promotional announcements

3. New hire announcements

4. Companies that are in trouble

5. Obituary notices

Each of these events suggests the possibility of newly created jobs.

Healthy, expanding companies typically have the need to hire from the outside to staff their growth and expansion. Companies experiencing difficulties may need to hire persons with specific knowledge and skills to help address their ills. Promotional announcements and obituary notices, on the other hand, may suggest the need to hire replacements at the current company, while new hire announcements may suggest the need for hiring replacements at former companies. All of these possibilities may warrant your attention if you are to fully capitalize on these potential job opportunities.

ADVERTISING RESPONSE

In order to fully tap the power of recruitment advertising, it is important that you know how to write an effective cover letter. The balance of this chapter is intended to assist you in analyzing recruitment advertising and helping you to prepare effective advertising response cover letters that will successfully market your skills and capabilities to prospective employers.

THE BEN FRANKLIN BALANCE SHEET

When analyzing an employment ad, a good process to use is the "Ben Franklin balance sheet" approach. To employ this method, simply draw a line down the middle of a sheet of paper. To the left of the line write the heading "Employer's Requirements." To the right of the line, insert the heading "My Qualifications."

Carefully read the employment advertisement, line by line, for each specific qualification (education, experience, personal traits, and so on) required by the employer. Delineate these to the left of the line under the heading "Employer's Requirements." Pay particular attention to those qualifications which the employer appears to be emphasizing. These should be listed first, with lesser qualifications following. Use of certain words or expressions (for example, "must have," "requires," and "prefer") in the ad will help you differentiate these important qualifications from those of less importance.

Now to the right of the line (under the heading "My Qualifications"), list your own personal qualifications that correspond to each of the employer's stated requirements. This will facilitate a direction comparison between the employer's specific needs and your own qualifications for the position advertised, and provide you with the basis for preparation of an effective advertising response cover letter.

TYPES OF COVER LETTERS

Essentially, when responding to employment advertising, there are two recommended approaches. These are:

1. Linear comparison approach

2. Narrative comparison approach

The linear comparison approach is recommended when you have *all* or *most* of the qualifications required in the ad. This approach makes use of a line-by-line listing of your qualifications, with each line corresponding to a specific qualifications requirement as stated in the ad.

Example

Careful review of your requirements suggests that I am well-qualified for the position of Materials Control Manager. Please consider the following:

1. *M.B.A. degree with materials management emphasis*
2. *15 years materials flow experience*
3. *3 years management with Fortune 200 company*
4. *Thoroughly trained in JIT applications*
5. *Well versed in "Total Quality" vendor certification methods*
6. *8 years experience in consumer products industry*

This linear comparison approach facilitates direct comparison with your qualifications, and serves to highlight just how closely your qualifications match the employer's requirements. It is extremely effective in leading the employer to the obvious conclusion that you are well-qualified and should be given strong consideration for the position.

The narrative comparison approach, on the other hand, is recommended when you have only *some* of the employer's requirements. Instead of the linear approach as previously described, this approach makes use of a narrative or literary technique in making the qualifications comparison. The narrative approach, unlike the linear approach, does not serve to highlight areas of qualification deficit, where such exist. The narrative technique makes such deficits less obvious, and is therefore recommended when not all requirements stated in the ad can be met.

Example

Your ad states that you are seeking a "Ph.D. statistician with over 10 years experience in the field of Total Quality." I hold a Ph.D. in Statistics from Washington University and have been employed by the Mifflin Company in the field of Total Quality for the last 12 years. Currently I am Manager of Total Quality for the company.

COMPONENTS—EFFECTIVE ADVERTISING RESPONSE COVER LETTER

As illustrated in the two sample letters contained at the end of this chapter, the key components of an effective advertising response cover letter are as follow:

1. *Introductory Paragraph*
   - Reference to advertisement
   - Publication date
   - Publicaton name
   - Title of position advertised
   - Statement of interest

2. *Second Paragraph* (Qualifications Comparison)
   - Comparison—your qualifications vs. employer's requirements
   - Use of linear *or* narrative approach

3. *Third Paragraph* (Request Meeting)
   - Reaffirmation statement of qualifications match
   - Expression of interest in meeting

4. *Fourth Paragraph* (How to Reach You)
   - Phone number(s)
   - Times to reach you

5. *Fifth Paragraph* (Close)

The following sample cover letters are provided as models to assist you in the preparation of effective advertising response cover letters that will serve to market your qualifications. You will notice how they effectively employ the components presented in the foregoing outline.

ADVERTISEMENT RESPONSE-LINEAR APPROACH

```
                                    122 Warren Drive
                                    West Bend, MI 18775
                                    February 22, 1994
```

```
Ms Sandra Willard
Director, Corporate Employment
Washington Paper Company
5000 Commerce Blvd.
Chicago, IL 30552
```

Dear Ms Willard:

Enclosed please find my resume in response to your recent advertisement in the February 21st edition of the <u>Chicago Tribune</u> for a Director of Total Quality. This position sounds exciting, and I would welcome the opportunity to discuss it with you during a personal meeting.

As my resume will attest, I would appear to have excellent qualifications for this position as follows:

1. Ph.D. in Statistics from University of Michigan.
2. Graduate of the W. Edwards Deming Institute - 1991.
3. Designed and successfully implemented corporate-wide total quality program at Hunt Foods.
4. Well versed in the application of statistical methods (i.e., design of experiments, control charting, variance analysis, etc.).
5. Trained over 5,000 hourly workers, operations managers, and engineers in statistical quality techniques (a 6 course program).

Should you agree that my background is a good match for your requirements, I would welcome the opportunity to meet with you to further explore this excellent opportunity. I feel confident that I can provide the kind of leadership that you are seeking for your company's total quality effort.

I can be reached during the day on a confidential basis at my office. My office number is (312) 776-0978.

Thank you for your consideration, and I look forward to hearing from you.

```
                                    Sincerely,
                                    David R. Whitburn
                                    David R. Whitburn
```

Enclosure

ADVERTISEMENT RESPONSE-NARRATIVE APPROACH

316 Willis Road
Grand Rapids, MI 32115
July 12, 1996

Mr. William Buttersworth
Engineering Manager
East River Paper Company
155 Old Paper Mill Road
Wawa, WI 87116

Dear Mr. Buttersworth:

Your advertisement in the July 12th issue of <u>Paper News</u> for a Project
Engineering - Converting has peaked my interest. This sounds like an
exciting opportunity that is in keeping with my current career goals,
and I am therefore enclosing my resume for your consideration. I think
you will find my qualifications an excellent match for your
requirements.

Your ad calls for a B.S. in Engineering with 3 or more years experience
in paper converting project engineering. You state that experience with
Wilson winders and Haysen wrappers is also desirable. I have a B.S. in
Mechanical Engineering from Central Michigan University and have 4 years
project experience with Weston Paper Company in converting engineering.
This experience has included the design modification, installation and
start-up of Wilson winders as well as the installation and start-up of
Haysen wrapper equipment.

As called for in your ad, I have worked independently on smaller project
assignments (up to $4 million) as well as a team member on larger
assignments (up to $25 million). I also have extensive control systems
experience, including Honeywell 3000 systems.

It would appear that I am well-qualified for the position of Project
Engineer - Converting, and I would welcome the opportunity to further
discuss this position with you and the members of your Engineering
Staff.

I can be reached, on a confidential basis, during the day at (313) 887-
9072 or at my home in the evening at (313) 886-9084.

Thank you for your consideration, and I look forward to hearing from
you.

Sincerely,

Bradley S. Davis

Enclosure

6

THE STRONG CASE FOR NETWORKING

What the Experts Say

E mployment networking, the art of using personal contacts and connections to find a job, has long been known to be a significant factor in finding jobs. Just how important networking is as a job-hunting source has been open to discussion and debate for quite some time.

Over the years, I have heard numerous estimates concerning the degree of importance of this key job hunting technique. Although virtually all knowledgeable employment professionals readily concede that networking is clearly the primary factor in finding jobs, the debate has always centered on just how much of a role it really plays. For the most part, the estimates that I have heard have ranged from 60% to 80%.

In an attempt to set the record straight, I recently conducted a survey of 9 of the largest U.S. outplacement consulting firms. These firms are well known, and are clearly some of the largest and most successful consultants in this field. The results of this survey appear in Table 6.1.

HOW JOBS ARE FOUND

Source	Challenger Gray & Christmas (A)	Drake Beam Morin (A)	Executive Assets Corp. (E)	Jannotta Bray & Assoc. (A)	King Chapman Broussard & Gallagher (A)	Lee Hecht Harrison (E)	Manchester (A)	Mainstream Access (E)	Right Assoc. (A)	Avg.
Networking (Personal Contact)	92%	65%	70%	62%	62%	82%	60%	65%	52%	68%
Search Firms and Employment Agencies	.8%	13%	20%	21%	14%	8%	17%	10%	19%	14%
Advertising	1%	11%	5%	10%	12%	7%	15%	12%	22%	10%
Direct Mail	0	3%	2%	7%	11%	3%	3%	1%	0	3%
Other	6.2%	8%	3%	0	1%	0	5%	12%	8%	5%
	100%	100%	100%	100%	100%	100%	100%	100%	100%	100%

(A) = Actual
(E) = Estimate

SURVEY FINDINGS

As you can see from the data reported by these major outplacement firms, networking (or personal contact) is by far
the most productive source of jobs, accounting on average
for some 68% of all positions found by the clients of these
consulting firms.

Going from high to low, the following were the networking results reported by each of these firms:

92% Challenger Gray & Christmas (Chicago)

82% Lee Hecht Harrison (New York City)

70% Executive Assets Corporation (Chicago)

65% Drake Beam Morin (New York City)

65% Mainstrean Access (New York City)

62% Jannotta Bray & Associates (Chicago)

62% King Chapman Broussard & Gallagher (Houston)

60% Manchester (Philadelphia)

52% Right Associates (Philadelphia)

You will note that search firms and employment agencies
are the next most effective job-hunting source, accounting
for 14% of the jobs, with advertising standing at 10%. Thus
networking, on the basis of these findings, accounts for
nearly 5 times as many jobs as its next closest competitor (search firms and employment agencies), and nearly 7
times as many jobs as its second closest competitor (advertising).

For the job seeker who wishes to find the right job
within 60 days these statistics should tell a pretty powerful
story. Obviously, networking needs to play a central role in
your job search strategy, if you have any real desire to successfully complete your job hunt within a reasonable time
frame.

OTHER IMPORTANT STUDIES

Although the evidence that I have just presented should in itself be rather convincing, there are 2 other studies that seem to confirm the validity of my findings. These are a 1975 study conducted by the United States Department of Labor, and a 1974 study conducted by Mark S. Granovetter, a Harvard University sociologist. As mentioned in Chapter 2, these studies may at first appear outdated. However, as we have already observed, there appears to be significant correlation. Let's briefly review the findings of these studies. (Note: Pie charts reflecting the results of these studies are contained in Chapter 2.)

Granovetter, whose study "Getting a Job: A Study of Contacts and Careers," was published by the Harvard University Press in 1974, conducted a sizeable study showing how professional, technical, and managerial persons found jobs. His data shows that a whopping 74.5% of the persons surveyed were successful in finding employment through personal contact (networking)!

The "runner up" source in Granovetter's survey was advertising, accounting for nearly 10% of all jobs. Thus, Granovetter's study shows that networking accounts for nearly 7.5 times more jobs than the second most productive job-hunting source (advertising). As a job seeker, this is not a differential to take lightly!

Another significant finding of the Granovetter Study was that a reported 43.8% of all jobs found through informal, personal contact (networking) were *newly created*, meaning that they did not formally exist as identified job openings prior to the networking contact being made. This is a very significant statistic that should really "hit home" for the serious job hunter!

Another finding of the Granovetter study should not go overlooked for those wanting to understand the importance of various job hunting sources. In his study, Granovetter reports that on average those jobs found through personal contact (networking) were found to be both "higher paying" and "more satisfying" than those found from other employment sources.

A 1975 study conducted by the United States Department of Labor also makes a strong point for the importance of networking as a job-hunting source. This study, entitled "Job-Seeking Methods Used by American Workers" and published in Bulletin #1886 by the Bureau of Labor Statistics, shows that 63.4% of all persons surveyed had found their jobs through informal personal contact (networking). This study is slightly different from the Granovetter Study and my own study, in as much as it includes both white and blue collar workers in its sample.

As with my own study, as well as Granovetter's, the Labor Department's study also reveals that personal contact (networking) accounts for significantly more jobs than any other job-hunting source. In the case of this study, for example, networking accounts for over 4.5 times the number of jobs found through the next closest source (advertising).

So, as you can see, networking is by far the most important and productive job-hunting source, far outstripping any other source of jobs. The 3 studies that I have presented here clearly show that it produces anywhere from 4.5 to 7.5 more jobs than the next most productive source. It should be clear then, that employment networking needs to be the centerfold of your job-hunting campaign!

WHAT THE EXPERTS SAY

Although I have already provided some pretty overwhelming evidence about the importance of networking to your job-hunting campaign, I thought you might like to hear what some of the nation's leading experts in the outplacement consulting field have to say about this important source. So, during the course of my survey of the 9 leading outplacement consulting firms, I asked for some comments from certain of their key officers and consultants.

Here is what they had to say:

Joseph A. Carter, Senior Vice President & General Manager—Manchester

(Note: Manchester, a Philadelphia-based outplacement consulting firm, is a major player in the outplacement field, employing over 50 consultants and having 11 offices in the Boston to Washington, D.C., corridor. This firm annually provides job search training and support to over 2,000 persons through their individual programs, and another 2,000 to 3,000 annually through their group outplacement programs.)

More than 70% of all effective job seekers find positions through systematic "networking," which is both the art and science of leveraging personal contacts in a geometric progression. In Manchester's experience, individuals who are willing and able to actively network find new positions in one-third the amount of time consumed by those who do not network. The objective of such an exercise is to engage in a series of creative conversations with people who can:

- Provide further information about an industry, company, or decision maker

- React to a few of your most important accomplishments and assist in validating the viability of your job search objective

- Suggest additional contacts to expand your original network

- Enable you to pursue the job that, perhaps, hasn't been created yet and, thus, become a 'population of one' in the consideration, thereby avoiding the intense competition of typical ad response and the complex/highly political search firm referral process

The effective networker learns how to identify the ideal target organizations for his/her services through systematic research and to penetrate these organizations one-on-one by determining how to best leverage personal contacts (sometimes through multiple levels) in order to reach the decision-maker who could hire him/her.

By breaking down information obtained through conversation with intermediaries or from library business directories about specific individuals, he/she discovers possible mutual acquaintances through identification of possible club members, professional and industry associations, colleges attended, memberships on corporate and charitable boards, hometowns, former company associations, etc. With each face-to-face visit, he/she brings a list of the companies he/she would like to penetrate and asks if the immediate contact knows anybody in these organizations. If so, he/she asks if they may call that person and indicate that they are doing so at the present contact's suggestion (not necessarily with insistence on personal recommendation or endorsement, but merely by way of introduction.)

The effective networker phones the intended target contact on a direct dial extension early in the morning, late in the day, or at 12:15 P.M. when a secretary is least likely to block the call and says something like the following: "Harry, this is John Smith of Apex Corporation, would you have a minute? I know you're very busy and I hope I'm not intruding. I'm calling at the suggestion of our mutual friend, Bill Jones, who indicated that you might be able to be helpful to me. I'll take about 30 seconds to get across.

I've been a Human Resources executive all my life and, as the result of a recent merger and downsizing, I'm in the process of making a transition to another organization. I would love to speak to you face-to-face for 20 minutes or so, not with the expectation that you have a suitable job there, or even know of one. But, rather, because of your long seasoning and stature as a respected professional in this business, I could benefit substantially from having a brief conversation with you and gaining the wisdom of your thoughts. I'd like to tell you about a few important things I've done and ask for your opinion on the viability of the target objective I have in mind. I can also share some intelligence with you about leading H.R. practices.

You may also be in a position to recommend a couple of others with whom I could have a creative conversation in an effort to meet as many people as possible and, thereby, ultimately uncover a situation which cries out for what I can do. I'd be happy to meet you anytime day or night at your convenience and will limit the meeting to 20 or 30 minutes. Would your calendar permit us to get together sometime in the next week or so?"

The effective networker opens the subsequent face-to-face meeting with a carefully presented 2-minute overview of who he/she is, what he/she has done in their career, and what his/her job objective is. The networker tries to obtain useful data for calibrating job search strategy as well as additional names to call in order to advance the campaign. All such meetings are followed up with personal thank you notes and possible periodically sent clipped articles of interest with informal buck-slip notes attached, as a way of providing a gentle reminder of the contact and an update on campaign progress.

While methodically pursuing key contacts in critical target organizations, the skilled networker does not ignore people of all types with whom he/she can network, and he/she becomes comfortable and confident in openly describing his/her traditional status. For those individuals who are introverted and find networking difficult or uncomfortable, they should start the process with close-in friends and family members. It should also be pointed out that some of the best contacts come from some of the humblest of sources. The point is to publicize widely one's ability, skills/interests and to do so in a manner that reflects professionalism, hope, and the full expectation of success.

Virginia M. Lord, Senior Vice President—Right Associates

(Note: Right Associates is one of the world's largest outplacement consulting firms. Based in Philadelphia, this firm has over 70 offices worldwide and employs over 500 consultants. On an annual basis, it provides job search consulting and training services to over 22,000 persons through both its individual and group programs.)

The old cliche "it's not what you know, but who you know" often proves true when you're engaged in the job search process. While "what you know"—the actual skills necessary for successful job performance—is certainly important, "who you know" is the factor most likely to ultimately land you a job.

As our figures show, most positions of quality are filled through informal means—networking. Managers will most often reach out to people they know to find out who might be available to fill a need or solve a problem. If you become known to such a grapevine, you will have access to these opportunities, and with very little competition. Failing to do so will mean that your campaign will be limited to the formal approaches often placing you in direct competition with 500 to 1,000 others.

Building a strong contact network is therefore the most important and valuable step in the job search process. A contact is not necessarily a person who can hire you or who knows of a position. He or she may also be a person who can help you get to an executive or knows enough about organizations in your field of interest to help you focus on your campaign, or provide other valuable information.

It is important to engage in mutually beneficial networking, which means getting not only what you want from a person, but also providing that person who helped you with some networking feedback from which they can benefit. It's a two-way process. Keep the lines of communication open and ongoing. Be sure to close all contacts originally supplied by the person. Such follow-up is essential, not only for those beginning a job search, but for everyone. While you may not be looking for a job now, future circumstances may necessitate that you do so and this is when an ongoing network of contacts is invaluable.

In closing, everyone has a contact network but its only as valuable as you make it. To keep your network productive, provide your contacts with an ongoing flow of good and relevant information.

Ronald S. Ross, Senior Principal—King Chapman & Broussard, Inc.

(Note: King Chapman & Broussard, a Houston-based outplacement consulting firm, is one of the largest career-transition consulting firms in the United States. With 10

offices from Los Angeles to New York City, this firm employs a staff of over 100 professionals. It provides job search training and support services to over 2,000 persons annually through its individual programs, and several thousand more through its group seminars and training programs.)

My personal observation over the past five years is that networking, *in its truest sense*, is responsible for perhaps eight/nine of ten jobs ... even when there is another source involved, i.e., an ad.

Even the best-intentioned company recordkeeping is questionable. It asks the wrong questions, leading to shaky assumptions. For example, consider the people who have claimed to find their new position exclusively through an advertisement. Scratch the assertion a bit more deeply and you might find that it was a call from a friend, someone in the network that pointed out the ad.

Perhaps it was just a call on the home answering machine saying, "Dick, did you see the ad in *The Wall Street Journal* for... ? Sounds just up your alley."

Someone sending out a direct mailing finds a name on the list they've not contacted in a long time; screws up the courage to call instead of write... and winds up with an appointment. Was it the discipline of the direct mailing? Does it really matter?

Historically, we have noted the candidates who take the longest to relocate are frequently the men and women who devote themselves unselfishly to the good of their former employer. Their networks were limited, shallow, and often only inside. It is when they are out in the open air of a job search that the realization strikes home; they are severely limited in a network of business/personal relationships at the very moment that they are most urgently needed.

Which has led those of us at KCB&G to the firm conviction that networking... *true networking* is more a matter of *authentic* life time alliances than the trivialized passing out of business cards and awkward stock form letters that goes by that name!

Even superb job skills will not protect someone in the economy of the 1990s. It is time devoted *daily to creating and maintaining* a personal network, by a willingness to be of service to others, that will in the final analysis, provide the only career flexibility/security!

Sheryl Spanier, Senior Consultant—Lee Hecht Harrison, Inc.

(Note: With 16 offices spread throughout major metropolitan areas in the East, Midwest, and the West Coast, Lee Hecht Harrison is one of the major outplacement consulting firms in the United States. Employing over 100 consultants, this firm offers a complete range of job search training and support programs to both groups and individual clients.)

Upon completing their job search campaigns, most of our clients report to us that they find that one very positive outcome of their experience is an increased appreciation of networking. Those individuals who come to us with a well-developed and nurtured contact base usually have a smoother transition. Their affiliations and reputations ease the way to new opportunities. By contrast, those people who have to learn how to network while at the same time going through a difficult career transition, can find the challenge somewhat overwhelming. After they are reestablished professionally, many commit themselves to expanding and maintaining a group of professional contacts as a career management tool in the future.

We define networking as a social process for a business purpose. Most of us use networking all the time—to gather information necessary to our jobs or conduct our daily personal lives. Simply put, networking is the method of developing relationships based on commonalities; seeking the advice and assistance of others in gathering information about an industry, a company, or a person; and creating partnerships with others to share information about trends and leads in a field of interest.

When applying networking to a career transition, some clients initially misperceive its impact. Some, afraid of rejection, want to limit their exposure; they are fearful of being seen as exploitative or reaching out for sympathy. Once they grasp the advantages of expanding visibility options, however, most outplaced executives discover that contacts, when asked about something they can do to help another individual, will gladly contribute.

Problems with networking usually occur when a job hunter goes through the motions of networking, hoping that just meeting someone and conducting a 15-minute interview, or passing along a resume, will automatically result in a job. Networking works best when it is based on building relationships and developing reciprocity.

Even when they do not get a job through a contact, our clients tell us that networking has helped them. When a person leaves a job, he loses not just a title and office; he loses his sense of affiliation, ongoing feedback and support regarding his worth in the marketplace, and a sense of structure in daily activities. Networking during a job search replaces some of these losses. By meeting with experts in one's field, a job seeker increases his visibility and knowledge, keeps current and connected regarding new developments and opportunities and continues to feel alive professionally. He then can go to an interview better prepared to understand the needs of a potential employer and with perspective and otherwise isolated candidate would not have.

So, regardless of how a position is found, networking enhances a job search. Further, once employed, an executive who engages in this process during a career transition can continue to grow professionally and will enhance his future options by staying connected, helping others, and expanding his contact base.

Now you have heard what some of the world's leading outplacement consulting experts have to say about the importance of employment networking as a job-hunting source. From this, as well as the studies discussed earlier in this chapter, I am sure that you have come to the realization that networking needs to play a key role in your job search process. This is particularly true if you want to successfully complete your job search within a reasonable time.

Let's now move on to the process of networking. The next few chapters will provide you with the training needed to become a proficient networker and to fully exploit this very important job search source.

7

GETTING PAST
THE SECRETARY

One of the first challenges that you will meet as you begin making your networking telephone calls is the challenge of getting past the targeted executive's secretary. Depending upon the secretary, this may sometimes prove to be a major task and require the use of some good strategy and tactics on your part. This chapter is intended to help you to prepare to effectively penetrate this barrier and to cultivate a relationship with the secretary that should prove beneficial to your networking objectives.

SECRETARY'S ROLE

In order to formulate a proper approach in effectively dealing with secretaries, you must first fully understand and appreciate the secretary's role in the handling of incoming telephone calls. Essentially, this role is twofold:

- Protector/Gatekeeper
- Helper/Facilitator

Well-trained secretaries realize that one of their important roles in supporting a busy boss is to field and fend off unimportant and unnecessary phone calls that could serve to waste the boss's time. Their roles are therefore to first determine whether or not the nature of the call is such that it really requires the boss to get involved at all. If there is no need to involve the boss, the secretary will normally field the call directly, attempting either to assist the caller personally or by referral of the call to an appropriate person within the organization who can provide meaningful assistance. In any event, the secretary will attempt, where appropriate, to protect the boss from unnecessary calls.

So a key role of an effective secretary is to serve as the telephone gatekeeper for the boss, shielding the boss from unnecessary calls and being protective of the boss's time. In this way the secretary ensures that the boss's time is closely guarded and efficiently used in attending to those things important to effective job performance and career success. Busy executives greatly appreciate this kind of protection and value the services of a good secretary who can effectively shield them from such calls.

On the other hand a second role of the secretary, when handling incoming telephone calls, is that of helper/facilitator. Once it has been determined that the incoming call is an important one requiring the boss's attention, the role of the secretary shifts from gatekeeper/protector to helper/facilitator. It now becomes the secretary's responsibility to help facilitate a direct discussion between the caller and the boss at the earliest opportunity, consistent, of course, with the boss's schedule and business priorities.

Highly efficient executive secretaries are always mindful of the value of their boss's time. Once determining that the incoming call is sufficiently important to warrant direct conversation with their boss, a good secretary will attempt to glean as much information from the caller as possible concerning the reason for the call. By providing the boss with a short briefing prior to taking the call, the secretary ensures that the boss is well-prepared for the conversation and can dispatch the caller following a brief but polite conversation. It will be very common for the secretary to ask you several probing questions concerning the nature of your call during your networking calls, and you will need to be prepared for this.

Part of being an effective helper/facilitator requires the secretary to also determine the relevant importance of the telephone call in the context of the boss's current schedule and work priorities. Care is taken to delay calls that could prove disruptive to current work priorities and the secretary will attempt to arrange for a return call at a time that is more convenient to the boss's schedule.

Thus, the effective secretary assumes the role of helper/ facilitator. Always mindful of the boss's schedule and work priorities, he or she must make certain decisions concerning the importance of the call in the context of current priorities, and decide whether it is appropriate to put the call through on an immediate basis or to arrange for a return call at a time that is more convenient. Secondly, in the interests of further conserving the boss's time, the secretary will provide the boss with as much information concerning the nature of the call as possible. Both of these services are much valued by busy managers and executives whose schedules require that they remain conscious of their time and priorities at all times.

SECRETARY—FRIEND OR FOE?

It is important to the success of your networking efforts to both understand and appreciate that the secretary can and will play a very key role. Effective sales persons have long appreciated the important role that a good secretary can play in the sales process. As a job seeker, you need to be keenly aware of this as well. The impression you create and rapport that you establish during your brief relationship with your target executive's personal secretary can clearly impact the results of your networking efforts with the secretary's boss.

If you are pleasant, considerate, and respectful of the secretary's role, you substantially improve the probabilities of a successful networking outcome. If rude or discourteous, on the other hand, you may never even have the opportunity to talk with the boss.

So, the decision is yours. You can befriend the secretary and secure him/her as a personal ally, or you can anger the secretary and turn him/her into a personal adversary. It's all up to you! An old adage seems appropriate at this point: "You can catch more flies with sugar than you can with vinegar." Why then use vinegar when you have a choice?

Treating a secretary with dignity and respect can clearly win you an important ally. If you are pleasant, polite, and acknowledge the validity and importance of their role, you can win a real friend, an ally who will frequently go the "extra mile" to be of assistance to you and your cause. It is critical to the success of your networking process, therefore, that you employ techniques that will build and reinforce a positive relationship with the target executive's secretary. This chapter is intended to help you do exactly that!

KEYS TO EFFECTIVE RELATIONSHIP

Before placing your call and making contact with the target executive's secretary, it is important to remind yourself that there are 3 important elements to creating an effective relationship with the secretary and to winning him/her over as your personal ally:

1. *Friendliness.* To establish yourself as someone who is pleasant and friendly—someone who it is easy to like and help.

2. *Respect.* To establish yourself as someone who is courteous and respectful—sensitive and appreciative of the secretary's role.

3. *Validity.* To establish that you have a valid and compelling need to speak directly with the boss.

How you approach the secretary, and what techniques you employ in managing this relationship, will be critical to meeting these objectives and achieving a desirable outcome to your networking efforts. Let's now take a look at some of these approaches and techniques.

Smiling

The tone of your voice is critical to establishing a positive image as someone who is pleasant and friendly—someone who is easy to like. If abrupt, curt, intense, serious, or condescending in your tone the result will be that you will be seen as unfriendly, detached, or aloof and the secretary will have considerably less motivation to assist you. By contrast, if you sound pleasant, warm, and friendly, chances are that you will elicit favorable feelings on the part of the secretary and noticeably improve his or her desire to assist you.

To improve your tone and enhance the probability of establishing a friendly relationship, I suggest that you physically force yourself to smile throughout your telephone conversation. You will find the results surprising!

As an experiment, try smiling and at the same time trying to say something unpleasant. For example, try smiling and at the same time saying, "I don't like you!" Pretty hard to do, isn't it? Despite the unpleasant nature of your message, it is practically impossible to sound unpleasant.

Now try reversing the process. Try frowning, turning the corners of your mouth down, and saying, "I like you!" Equally difficult, isn't it?

Similar experiments have led some outplacement experts to strongly recommend that job seekers place a mirror in front of them prior to making networking telephone calls. By using the mirror to periodically check your facial expressions throughout the networking call, and by continuously focusing on smiling throughout your conversation, the effect can be dramatic. You will find that this technique greatly affects the tone of your voice, causing you to come across as a very warm, friendly, and positive person.

So, remember—when you pick up the phone—smile! Try to reach the point that smiling becomes automatic.

Overcoming Common Barriers and Objections

In effectively managing your relationship with secretaries during the networking process, you will need to prepare yourself to overcome several common barriers and objections frequently encountered by the job seeker during the networking process. These roadblocks are in the form of various common questions and statements made by the secretary. To be effective at networking you must be fully prepared to address and successfully overcome these obstacles.

The balance of this chapter is committed to describing these common roadblocks and introducing you to various techniques that can be effectively used to remove these obstacles and achieve the objective of speaking directly with your targeted contacts. These barriers are presented in pretty much the sequence that you will likely encounter during the course of your conversation with the secretary.

First Stage Barrier—Executive Not Available The first barrier normally encountered during the networking call is that the target executive is simply not available to speak with you. Typically the secretary will provide a brief explanation of the reason for his or her boss's inaccessibility as follows:

> I'm sorry, Mr. Jones is out of the office today.
>
> I'm sorry, Mr. Jones is unavailable at the moment.
>
> I'm sorry, Mr. Jones is in a meeting.
>
> I'm sorry, Mr. Jones is unable to talk with you at the moment.
>
> Mr. Jones is tied up and will have to get back to you.
>
> I'm sorry, Mr. Jones is currently out to lunch.
>
> I'm sorry, Mr. Jones is traveling today.
>
> I'm sorry, Mr. Jones is on vacation.

Regardless of the reason stated for the targeted executive's unavailability, your line of inquiry needs to establish two things:

1. When the executive will be available to take your call.
2. What time is best to make contact.

The following mini-dialogues will illustrate how to effectively counter these temporary roadblocks posed by the secretary:

SCENARIO #1: (He's out of the office)

Secretary: Hello, Mr. Jones' office.

You: Hello, this is Sally Johnson. With whom am I speaking?

Secretary: Linda Robinson, Mr. Jones' secretary.

You: Ms. Robinson, is Mr. Jones available?
Secretary: I'm sorry, Mr. Jones is out of the office.
You: I see. When is he expected to return?
Secretary: He's not expected back until Friday morning.
You: What does his schedule look like for Friday? Would there be a good time to reach him?
Secretary: Well, he has an all-morning meeting, but you might try early afternoon.
You: Thank you Ms. Robinson, I will try then.
Secretary: You're quite welcome.

SCENARIO #2: (He's in a meeting)

Secretary: Hello, Mr. Jones' office.
You: Hello, this is Sally Johnson. Is Mr. Jones available?
Secretary: I'm sorry, he's in a meeting.
You: With whom am I speaking?
Secretary: This is Mr. Jones' secretary, Linda Robinson.
You: Ms. Robinson, would there be a good time to reach him later today?
Secretary: Yes, it looks as though he will be free at about 3:00 o'clock.
You: Thank you, Ms. Robinson. I will try then.
Secretary: You're welcome.

SCENARIO #3: (He's unavailable at the moment)

Secretary: Hello, Mr. Jones' office.
You: Hello, this is Sally Johnson calling. Is Mr. Jones in?
Secretary: I'm sorry, Mr. Jones is unavailable at the moment.
You: I see. With whom am I speaking?
Secretary: This is Linda Robinson. I'm Mr. Jones' Administrative Assistant.

You:	I see, Ms. Robinson. When might be a good time to reach Mr. Jones?
Secretary:	Well, he has a pretty heavy schedule today. You might try tomorrow morning.
You:	What time would you suggest I call in the morning?
Secretary:	A good time to reach him is between 7:00 and 8:00 A.M. He usually comes in early to read his mail and get some work done before starting the normal workday.
You:	Thank you, Ms. Robinson. I will plan to call him then.
Secretary:	You're very welcome.

SCENARIO #4: (He's unable to talk with you at the moment)

Secretary:	Hello, Linda Robinson speaking.
You:	Hello, this is Sally Johnson calling. Is this Mr. Jones' office?
Secretary:	Yes it is, but he is unable to talk with you at the moment.
You:	I see, Ms. Robinson. When would you suggest that I reach him?
Secretary:	A good time to contact him would be between 4:00 and 5:00 P.M. today.
You:	Thank you, Ms. Robinson. I will call back then.
Secretary:	You're welcome.

SCENARIO #5: (He's tied up and will have to get back to you)

| *Secretary:* | Hello, Mr. Jones' office. This is Linda Robinson speaking. |
| *You:* | Hello, this is Sally Johnson calling. May I speak with Mr. Jones please? |

Secretary: Gee, I'm sorry, but he's tied up at the moment and will have to get back to you.

You: I see. Well, perhaps it might be easier for me to call back later. When might be a good time to reach him?

Secretary: I might suggest later today, around 3:30 P.M. or so.

You: It looks like I'm going to be out of the office at 3:30, Ms. Robinson. What does his schedule look like tomorrow?

Secretary: He will be on vacation tomorrow, but back in on Friday.

You: I see. When would be a good time to call Friday?

Secretary: I would suggest about 10:30 A.M.

You: Good. I will plan to call him then. Thank you, Ms. Robinson.

Secretary: You're quite welcome.

SCENARIO #6: (He's out to lunch)

Secretary: Hello, Mr. Jones' office. May I help you?

You: Yes, this is Sally Johnson calling. May I speak to Mr. Jones please?

Secretary: Sally, I'm sorry, but Mr. Jones is at lunch at the moment.

You: I see. With whom am I speaking?

Secretary: This is Linda Robinson, Mr. Jones' secretary.

You: I see. Linda, when might be a good time to reach Mr. Jones?

Secretary: You might try about 2:00 this afternoon. He should be between meetings and in his office.

You: Thank you, Linda, I'll try to reach him then.

Secretary: You're welcome.

SCENARIO #7: (He's traveling today)

Secretary:	Good morning, Mr. Jones' office.
You:	Good morning, this is Sally Johnson calling. Is Mr. Jones there?
Secretary:	I'm sorry, Mr. Jones is traveling on business today.
You:	I see. With whom am I speaking?
Secretary:	This is Linda Robinson.
You:	Linda, when do you expect Mr. Jones to return? Is there a good time to reach him?
Secretary:	He should be back on Thursday. You might try then.
You:	I see. What does his Thursday schedule look like? Is there a time that you might suggest I call?
Secretary:	You might try about 9:00 A.M. His first meeting starts at 9:30.
You:	Thank you, Linda. I'll try reaching him on Thursday at 9:00 A.M.
Secretary:	You're welcome.

SCENARIO #8: (He's on vacation)

Secretary:	Hello, may I help you?
You:	Yes, is this Mr. Jones' office?
Secretary:	Yes it is.
You:	This is Sally Johnson calling. May I speak with Mr. Jones please?
Secretary:	I'm sorry, but Mr. Jones is on vacation at the moment.
You:	I see. With whom am I speaking?
Secretary:	This is Ms. Robinson. I'm Mr. Jones' secretary.
You:	Ms. Robinson, when is Mr. Jones expected back from vacation?
Secretary:	Not until the 15th.

You:	Ms. Robinson, when would you suggest I try to reach him?
Secretary:	He has a pile of work waiting for him and several meetings scheduled on the 15th and 16th. I believe I would wait until Monday, the 19th.
You:	Would there be a good time on Monday to reach him?
Secretary:	It's really hard to say at this point.
You:	I can appreciate that. Why don't I plan to call you at 9:00 A.M. on the 19th and check his schedule at that time.
Secretary:	That sounds like a good idea to me, Ms. Johnson.
You:	Good. I'll plan to speak with you then. Thank you, Ms. Robinson.
Secretary:	You're quite welcome.

Review of these scenarios reveals some common elements which it is suggested that you utilize when encountering this first step barrier (executive not available). These elements are the following:

1. In your opening statement, always introduce yourself by name. This eliminates the need for the secretary to ask who is calling. Additionally, using your name may suggest that Mr. Jones knows you.

    Example: Hello, this is Sally Johnson. May I speak with Mr. Jones please?

2. If not volunteered, ask the secretary his/her name. Use of the secretary's name during the call "personalizes" the call and shows that you have interest in her/him as a person. Too often secretaries are treated as inanimate objects, a sort of "robot" that is there simply to be of service.

Example: With whom am I speaking?...I see. Ms. Robinson, when do you expect Mr. Jones will return?... Thank you, Ms. Robinson, I will plan to call Mr. Jones on Friday at 9:00 A.M.

3. Establish when Mr. Jones will be available, thus increasing the probability of making contact and ensuring most effective use of your time.

   Example: Ms. Robinson, when would you suggest I contact Mr. Jones?

4. Establish a specific time when it will be best to reach Jones.

   Example: What does his schedule look like on Wednesday, Ms. Robinson? What would be the best time to call?

5. A little bit of courtesy goes a long way. Always remember to thank the secretary for his or her assistance.

   Example: Thank you, Ms. Robinson. I will call back then.

6. Although the secretary may offer to have Jones call you back, on very important contacts it is always better to take the initiative and offer to call back instead. In this way you will not be caught off-guard and will be better prepared to maximize the contact. Additionally, you can better control the timing of the call, being sure that your conversation is not rushed due to some other scheduled event.

7. Where comfortable, call the secretary by his or her first name. This tends to "personalize" rather than "formalize" the relationship. Take your lead from how the secretary introduces him or herself. If the secretary intro-

duces herself as Linda Robinson, call her "Linda." If she introduces herself as Ms. Robinson, however, it's probably better to address her as "Ms. Robinson."

Second Stage Barrier—Who Are You?   Early in most conversations, the secretary will attempt to find out the nature of your relationship with his or her boss. If there is a personal relationship or professional business relationship, the secretary is likely to put your call through to the targeted executive. On the other hand, should the secretary establish that it is a "cold call" (that is, no personal or business relationship), there is a substantially increased probability that your call will be "screened out," and you will not have the opportunity to talk directly with your targeted contact. In such cases the secretary will likely take one of the following 3 approaches:

1. Offer to assist you directly, without referring on to the boss.

2. Offer to discuss the matter with his/her boss and get back to you.

3. Suggest that you contact someone else in the organization (usually the Personnel or Employment Manager), who can "better assist you."

Anyone who is knowledgeable of the employment networking process knows that it is imperative to have direct dialogue with the targeted executive. Calls that are handled directly by the secretary or the personnel department almost never have a positive outcome. At best, you can normally expect a polite "kissoff"—thanking you for your inquiry, but advising you that there are no openings currently available that are suitable to your particular qualifications.

Wherever possible, therefore, it is extremely important that you avoid "cold calls" and use your networking skills to develop contacts who you can use as "referrals" when contacting your targeted executive.

The following questions are typical of those used by secretaries to qualify you as someone having the "right" to talk with their boss. These are aimed at establishing the nature of your relationship with his or her boss and determining whether there is any personal or professional obligation that would compel the boss to have dialogue with you.

1. Is Mr. Jones expecting your call?

2. Does Mr. Jones know you?

3. Are you acquainted with Mr. Jones?

4. May I ask how you know Mr. Jones?

5. Will Mr. Jones recognize your name?

6. May I ask the nature of your relationship with Mr. Jones?

Clearly you will need to penetrate these preliminary defenses if you are going to get through to your targeted contact. The following scenarios will provide you with some effective techniques for doing so.

SCENARIO #1: (Is he expecting your call?)

Secretary: Hello, Mr. Jones' office.

You: Hello, this is Sally Johnson. Is Mr. Jones available please?

Secretary: Ms. Johnson, is Mr Jones expecting your call?

You: No, but I have been referred to him by Doug Wilson, a mutual business associate.

Secretary: Just a moment, Ms. Johnson, and I will see if he can take your call.

You: Thank you.

SCENARIO #2: (Does he know you?)

Secretary:	Hello, Linda Robinson.
You:	Hello, is this Dave Jones' office?
Secretary:	Yes it is.
You:	This is Sally Johnson calling. Is Dave in?
Secretary:	Does Mr. Jones know you?
You:	No, not directly. However, Stephen Temple, a mutual friend of ours, suggested I give Dave a call.
Secretary:	I see. Let me see if Mr. Jones can speak with you. Just a moment.
You:	Thank you, Linda.

SCENARIO #3: (Are you acquainted with Mr. Jones?)

Secretary:	Hello, Mr. Jones' office.
You:	Hello, with whom am I speaking?
Secretary:	This is Ms. Robinson, Mr. Jones' administrative assistant.
You:	Ms. Robinson, is Mr. Jones available?
Secretary:	Are you acquainted with Mr. Jones?
You:	Only indirectly. I was referred to him by Allen Simpson, a colleague who knows Mr. Jones from their association as Board Members of the American Marketing Association. Allen suggested I give Mr. Jones a call.
Secretary:	Just a moment, Ms. Johnson, I will see if Mr. Jones can take your call.
You:	Thank you.

SCENARIO #4: (How do you know Mr. Jones?)

Secretary:	Hello, Mr. Jones' office. May I help you?
You:	Yes, this is Sally Johnson, may I speak with David please?

Secretary:	May I ask how you know Mr. Jones?
You:	Surely. With whom am I speaking?
Secretary:	This is Linda Robinson, Mr. Jones' secretary.
You:	Linda, David and I attended the University of Pennsylvania together and have known one another professionally for a number of years.
Secretary:	Just a moment, Ms. Johnson, and I'll put you through to Mr. Jones.
You:	Thank you. I appreciate your assistance.

SCENARIO #5: (Will Mr. Jones recognize your name?)

Secretary:	Hello, this is Linda Robinson speaking.
You:	Hello, Linda, this is Sally Johnson calling. May I speak with Mr. Jones please?
Secretary:	Will Mr. Jones recognize your name?
You:	No, but I was referred to him by a John Simpson, a close friend of mine.
Secretary:	Will Mr. Jones know Mr. Simpson?
You:	Yes, I understand they have done a lot of sailing together on the Chesapeake.
Secretary:	Just a moment please, and I'll see if he can take your call.
You:	Thank you, Linda.

SCENARIO #6: (May I ask the nature of your relationship with Mr. Jones?)

Secretary:	Hello, Mr. Jones' office. Linda Robinson speaking.
You:	Hello, Linda. This is Sally Johnson calling. Is Mr. Jones in?
Secretary:	Yes, he is. May I ask the nature of your relationship with Mr. Jones?

You:	Yes, Mr. Jones and I are professional acquaintances through the Delaware Manufacturers' Association.
Secretary:	I see. Let me check and see if he is available.
You:	Thank you, Linda.

Review of these mini dialogues shows how to answer the "who are you" questions in such as way as to legitimize your "right" to have direct conversation with your targeted executive, the secretary's boss. Establishing your relationship, either directly or indirectly (through others), with the boss suggests to the secretary that there is either a personal or professional obligation for the boss to accept the call. In most all such cases, the secretary will agree to put your call through.

You will note the various descriptions that can be used to describe your connection with the secretary's boss. These include:

Indirect Relationship

1. Referred by a mutual business associate

2. Referred by a mutual friend

3. Referred by a close friend

4. Referred by a fellow member of a professional society

Direct Relationship

1. A personal friend

2. A professional acquaintance

When preparing to answer the secretary's inquiries concerning "who you are," you should practice using these descriptions of your personal or professional relationship to categorize "who you are" and your relationship with his or her boss. Once the nature of this relationship has been communicated to the secretary, it will be nearly impossible for the secretary not to put your call through to his or her boss. This is because there is no way for the secretary to independently judge the value of these relationships. This is something only his or her boss can do. You have thus succeeded in removing the decision from his or her domain, and elevated it to the boss's level.

Third Stage Barrier—Why Are You Calling? Once the secretary has determined that you have a legitimate "right" to talk to the boss, on the basis of your personal or professional relationship, the secretary may elect to further qualify your call by inquiring as to the reason for your call. The reasons for such further qualification are:

1. To determine whether he or she can be of help without getting the boss directly involved.

2. To determine whether there is someone else in the organization who can better assist you.

3. To acquire sufficient information regarding the reason for your call, so the boss can be appropriately briefed before taking or returning your call.

Here are some different ways the secretary may elect to choose in requesting this information from you:

1. Will Mr. Jones know what this call is about?

2. May I ask what this call is in reference to?

3. Why should I tell Mr. Jones you are calling?

4. What is the nature of this call?

5. May I inquire why you are calling?

6. Is this a personal or a business call?

7. Why do you wish to speak with Mr. Jones?

Regardless of the way in which this "why are you call-ing" question is asked, it is one more attempt by the sec-retary to "screen out" unwanted calls and save the boss's valuable time. If you can't get by this one, you will once again be thwarted in your efforts to make direct contact with your targeted executive, and your networking efforts will end up on the rocks, in danger of sinking.

The following mini dialogues are offered to illustrate how you might effectively counter this additional barrier and still successfully "bag your quarry."

SCENARIO #1: **(Will Mr. Jones know what this call is about?)**

Secretary: Hello, Mr. Jones' office.

You: Hello, this is Sally Johnson calling. Is Mr. Jones available please?

Secretary: Yes, Ms. Johnson. Will Mr. Jones know what this call is about?

You: No, but I have been referred to him by Jeffrey Morse, a mutual friend of ours.

Secretary: Okay, Ms. Johnson, let me see if he is available.

You: Thank you.

SCENARIO #2: **(May I ask what this call is in reference to?)**

Secretary: Hello, Linda Robinson.

You: Hello Linda, is this Mr. Jones' office?

Secretary: Yes it is.

You: This is Sally Johnson calling. Is Mr. Jones in?

Secretary: Yes. May I ask what this call is in reference to?

You: I am calling at the suggestion of Chris Beatty, a mutual business associate. Chris felt that Mr. Jones might be in a position to offer me some professional advice on a particular matter.

Secretary: What type of matter, Ms. Johnson?

You: I would like to ask him to share some of his observations about current conditions in the steel industry, and would appreciate his general thoughts concerning a career shift that I am contemplating. Chris felt he could be particularly helpful to me in this regard, and I would really appreciate a few minutes of his time.

Secretary: Ms. Johnson, let me see if he can take your call.

You: Thank you, Linda. I really appreciate your help.

SCENARIO #3: **(Why should I tell Mr. Jones you are calling?)**

Secretary: Hello, Mr. Jones' office. Linda Robinson speaking.

You: Good morning, Linda. This is Sally Johnson calling. Is Mr. Jones available?

Secretary: Yes, he is. Is he expecting your call?

You: No, but Peggy Temple, a mutual friend, suggested I call him.

Secretary: I see. Why should I tell Mr. Jones you are calling?

You: Peggy told me that Mr. Jones is very knowledgeable about the steel industry and could give me some good advice.

Secretary: Ms. Johnson, what type of advice do you need? Perhaps I could help you.

You: Thank you, Linda, I appreciate the offer, but I am seeking some career advice, and Chris

	felt Mr. Jones might be in a position to suggest some key people in the industry whom I should contact.
Secretary:	I see, Ms. Johnson. Let me see if Mr. Jones can take your call.
You:	Thank you, Linda.

SCENARIO #4: (What is the nature of this call?)

Secretary:	Hello, Mr. Jones' office.
You:	Hello. With whom am I speaking?
Secretary:	This is Linda Robinson, Mr. Jones' administrative assistant.
You:	Good morning, Linda, this is Sally Johnson calling. May I please speak with Mr. Jones?
Secretary:	Will he recognize your name?
You:	Yes, we serve on the Board of the American Manufacturers' Association together.
Secretary:	Mr. Jones has a very busy schedule right now. What is the nature of this call?
You:	It's nothing urgent, Linda. I respect Dave's knowledge of the steel industry and wanted to ask him a few questions.
Secretary:	I see. What did you need to know?
You:	Well, quite frankly, I'm considering a career change, Linda, and would welcome his thoughts. I certainly don't expect that he will be aware of a specific job opportunity. I would, however, welcome his general thoughts concerning my approach to my job search.
Secretary:	Let me see what I can do. Just a moment please.
You:	Thank you, Linda.

SCENARIO #5: (May I inquire why you are calling?)

Secretary: Hello, Mr. Jones' office. May I help you?

You: Yes, with whom am I speaking?

Secretary: This is Ms. Robinson, Mr. Jones' administrative assistant.

You: Good afternoon, Ms. Robinson, this is Sally Johnson calling. May I please speak with Mr. Jones?

Secretary: Are you acquainted with Mr. Jones?

You: Only indirectly. I was referred to him by my cousin, Jim Johnson. They are both in Rotary together.

Secretary: I see. May I inquire why you are calling?

You: Yes, Ms. Robinson. I know he is very knowledgeable of the steel industry and I have some questions I would like to ask him.

Secretary: Could you be more specific, Ms. Johnson? What do you need to know?

You: I am in the process of making a career change and would appreciate his broad overview of the industry. I certainly don't expect him to be aware of specific openings for me. Perhaps he could share his thoughts about segments of the industry I should target, companies that are expanding, or key persons with whom I should be in contact. I would very much appreciate a few minutes of his time.

Secretary: Let me see if he has time to take your call, Ms. Johnson.

You: If not, I would be glad to call back at a more convenient time.

Secretary: Let me see.

You: Thank you, Ms. Robinson.

SCENARIO #6: (Is this a personal or a business call?)

Secretary:	Hello, Linda Robinson.
You:	Good morning, Linda. This is Sally Johnson calling. May I speak with Mr. Jones please?
Secretary:	Is he expecting your call?
You:	No, but please tell him that I am calling at the suggestion of Bill Worthington. He and Bill are tennis partners at the Oakborne Racket Club.
Secretary:	Is this a personal or a business call?
You:	Actually, Linda, it's both. I am calling to request both some personal and some business advice.
Secretary:	I see, Sally. What type of personal and business advice are you seeking?
You:	I am making a career change and would appreciate some general advice concerning conditions in the paper industry. Bill tells me that Mr. Jones is very knowledgeable of the industry and would be a good person to contact for some general advice on this subject.
Secretary:	Let me see if he is available.
You:	I appreciate your help, Linda.

SCENARIO #7: (Why do you wish to speak with Mr. Jones?)

Secretary:	Hello, David Jones' office. This is Linda speaking.
You:	Hello, Linda, this is Sally Johnson calling. Is Mr. Jones there please?
Secretary:	Does Mr. Jones know you, Sally?
You:	Yes, we went to Bucknell University together.
Secretary:	May I ask why you wish to speak with Mr. Jones?

You:	Yes, Linda, I would like to seek his general advice regarding a career change that I am making. Please assure him that I am not asking his help in finding me a job. I really don't expect that he will be aware of specific opportunities. What I really need is some general advice concerning conditions in the steel industry and some of his thoughts concerning my job search strategy. I would very much appreciate a few minutes of his time.
Secretary:	Okay, Sally, let me see what I can do.
You:	Thank you, Linda.

In general, it does not pay to be devious when answering the secretary's questions concerning "why you are calling." To do so simply generates mistrust and suggests to the secretary that you are attempting to hide something. Under these circumstances the secretary will feel uncomfortable, at best, about forwarding your call on to his or her boss. Clearly, early warning flags will go up, and the secretary may elect to "screen out" your call rather than to forward it and cause an uncomfortable situation for the boss.

As was shown in these preceding mini dialogues, you might try a simple, but honest answer first (for example, "I am calling to discuss some of his general observations concerning the condition of the steel industry, and to ask his advice on a matter"). If you are pressed to be more specific, however, it's time to "ante up" and to tell the secretary exactly why you need to speak with Jones.

You will note in reviewing the content of these scenarios, that when answering the secretary's question, "Why are you calling?", there are some good guidelines to follow. These are:

1. Never tell the secretary that you are "looking for a job." (It's okay, however, to say you are "contemplating or considering a career change.")

2. Always indicate that you are simply seeking general advice and ideas.

3. Stress that you are certainly not expecting his/her boss to be aware of specific job opportunities for you.

4. Where appropriate, use the name of your contact to subtly create a sense of personal or professional obligation for the boss to talk with you.

    Example: Bill suggested that Mr. Jones would be an excellent person to talk with regarding this matter.

5. Be polite, and always thank the secretary for his or her help.

Fourth Stage Barriers   Fourth stage barriers are always the most difficult to handle, and will require a little more creativity on your part. At this point you have gotten through the initial introduction, the "who are you" and the "why are you calling" routines, but the secretary, for some reason, is still reluctant to put your call through. There must be a reason for this. Either you haven't been very effective in your initial presentation, or there is something else standing in the way.

Here are some of the remaining barriers you may need to learn to overcome if you are going to be successful in getting to your targeted contact:

1. Mr. Jones doesn't take personal calls.

2. Mr. Jones does not take calls of this nature.

3. Company policy does not allow employees to take personal calls.

4. I think you need to talk to our personnel department; they handle all employment matters.

5. Mr. Jones does not provide job-hunting assistance.

6. Mr. Jones has an extremely busy schedule, and will not be able to talk with you.

7. Please send Mr. Jones your resume, and I'm sure that he will be glad to review it.

8. Mr. Jones has suggested that you contact George Lawton, our employment manager.

The following mini dialogues will illustrate some techniques that can be used to counter these remaining objections.

SCENARIO #1A: (He doesn't take personal calls.)

Secretary:	Hello, Mr. Jones' office.
You:	Hello, who am I speaking with?
Secretary:	This is Linda Robinson. I'm Mr. Jones' secretary.
You:	Linda, this is Sally Johnson calling. Is Mr. Jones in please?
Secretary:	Is he expecting your call?
You:	No, but I'm calling at the suggestion of Dawn Marks, a friend of Mr. Jones.
Secretary:	May I ask the nature of your call?
You:	Yes, Dawn tells me that Mr. Jones is very knowledgeable of the pharmaceutical industry, and I would like to see if he could share some of his observations with me about current opportunities in the industry.
Secretary:	I see. Well, I'm sorry, Ms. Johnson, but Mr. Jones doesn't take personal calls.
You:	Doesn't take personal calls? Linda, could you be more specific?

Secretary:	Yes. He doesn't like to take personal calls at the office.
You:	Oh, I see. If this is the case, would you check with him and see if I might call him at home this evening? Or perhaps he would prefer me to call later in the week.
Secretary:	Well, I don't know. Let me check with him.
Secretary:	Hello, Ms. Johnson, Mr. Jones says that he will speak with you this evening.
You:	Thank you, Linda. Do you have his home phone?
Secretary:	Yes, it's 446-8578.
You:	Thank you for your help, Linda. I'll call him this evening.

SCENARIO #1B: **(He doesn't take personal calls.) (This is a variation of the dialogue shown in 1A.)**

Secretary:	I see. Well, Ms. Johnson, I'm very sorry but Mr. Jones doesn't take personal calls.
You:	Doesn't take personal calls, Linda? Can you be more specific?
Secretary:	Yes, he's a very busy man and simply will not take personal calls.
You:	I see. That's too bad, I was looking forward to talking with him. Do you think I might call him at home this evening, or later in the week if tonight is not convenient?
Secretary:	I don't think so, Ms. Johnson.
You:	I see. What would you suggest I do?
Secretary:	I don't know. Perhaps you might want to send him a letter.
You:	That's a good thought. Perhaps I should do that. Thank you, Linda, for your help.

Note: At this point, you might also want to get back to your contact, Dawn Marks, for some advice. Depending on her relationship with Jones, she might be willing to intercede on your behalf and call Jones directly.

SCENARIO #2: (He doesn't take calls of this nature.)

Secretary: Hello, Mr. Jones' office. Linda Robinson speaking.

You: Good morning, Linda. This is Sally Johnson calling. May I speak with Mr. Jones please?

Secretary: Will he recognize your name, Sally?

You: No, but please tell him that I was referred to him by Dick Haviland.

Secretary: Ms. Johnson, may I inquire as to why you are calling?

You: Yes. Dick tells me that Mr. Jones is very knowledgeable of the paper industry and I wanted to ask his advice on a particular matter.

Secretary: What type of matter?

You: Well, Linda, I am contemplating a career change and would like the opportunity to discuss some of his thoughts and ideas regarding my job search. Don't misunderstand, Linda, I am not looking for a job, nor do I expect that Mr. Jones would be aware of one. But, I would appreciate a few minutes of his time to see if he may have some creative ideas on the subject. Dick Haviland says that he is very knowledgeable of the paper industry, and could have some good ideas on this subject.

Secretary: I'm sorry, Ms. Johnson, but Mr. Jones will not take calls of this nature.

You: Linda, could you be more specific?

Secretary: I don't know how to be more specific. He simply prefers not to take calls from persons looking for jobs.

You:	I see. Well, I'm sorry to hear that. I was really looking forward to talking with Mr. Jones, since Dick speaks so highly of him and his knowledge of the industry. Since I'm not looking for a job, but am only seeking his general observations concerning the state of the paper industry as it relates to my career change, do you feel perhaps he may make an exception?
Secretary:	Ms. Johnson, I really don't think so. He is pretty adamant on this subject.
You:	I see. Do you have other thoughts or ideas on this matter?
Secretary:	Not really.
You:	Well, perhaps I will still plan to drop him a line on this subject. Thank you, Linda.

Note: This is an absolute dead end. There is no point in pushing the matter further on a direct basis. Perhaps a good idea is to discuss the matter further with your mutual contact, Dick Haviland. Dick may have some further thoughts on the matter, or may decide to intercede directly with Jones on your behalf.

SCENARIO #3: (Company policy does not allow employees to take personal calls.)

Secretary:	Hello, this is Linda Robinson speaking. May I help you?
You:	Hello, Linda. This is Sally Johnson calling. Is Henry Jones in please?
Secretary:	Yes he is. Is this a personal call?
You:	Yes, it is. I was referred to him by Tom Murphy.
Secretary:	I'm very sorry, Ms. Johnson, but company policy does not allow employees to take calls of a personal nature.

You:	I see. Perhaps I could plan to call Mr. Jones at home in the evening.
Secretary:	That would be a good idea.
You:	Do you happen to have his home number, Linda?
Secretary:	I do, but I'm not allowed to release it without his permission.
You:	I understand. Could you please tell him that I was referred to him by a mutual business associate, Tom Murphy, and see if it would be alright for me to call him at home.
Secretary:	Just a moment. I'll check.
You:	Thank you, Linda.
Secretary:	Yes, call him this evening at 8:00 P.M. His home number is 366-2076.
You:	Thank you for your help, Linda.
Secretary:	You're quite welcome.

Note: With this approach, you have shown that you respect company policy and do not want to place the secretary in an uncomfortable position. You were able to overcome the barrier, however, by asking to speak to your targeted contact outside of business hours.

SCENARIO #4: (You need to talk with our personnel department. They handle all employment matters.)

Secretary:	Hello, Mr. Jones' office.
You:	Hello, with whom am I speaking?
Secretary:	This is Linda Robinson.
You:	Good morning, Linda. This is Sally Johnson calling. May I speak with Henry Johnson please?
Secretary:	Do you work for Zebar Company?
You:	No, I was referred to Mr. Jones by a mutual friend, Scott Beatty.
Secretary:	I see. Ms. Johnson, why do you wish to speak with Mr. Jones?

You:	Scott tells me that he is very knowledgeable of the food industry and would be a good person to contact for some general career advice.
Secretary:	Oh, if you're interested in employment, I know that Mr. Jones will want me to refer directly to our personnel department. They handle all matters pertaining to employment. Let me transfer you.
You:	Actually, Linda, I don't believe that the personnel department will be able to provide me with the kind of help that I am looking for. I am not looking for a job. What I am looking for is some broad advice and counsel concerning what is currently happening in the food industry. Scott Beatty seemed to feel that Mr. Jones would be an ideal person for me to talk with in this regard.
Secretary:	I see. Let me see if Mr. Jones is available to take your call.
You:	Thank you, Linda.

Note: In this scenario, you can see how easy it is to redirect the focus back to Jones from the personnel department by making it clear that you are seeking advice and counsel, not a job. You will also note how your need to talk directly with Jones was further reinforced through the use of your personal referral, Scott Beatty. Under these circumstances, it would be most difficult for the secretary to continue to insist that you talk to the personnel department.

SCENARIO #5: (He doesn't provide job-hunting assistance.)

Secretary:	Hello, this is Linda Robinson.
You:	Hello, Linda. This is Sally Robinson calling. Is Mr. Jones in please?

Secretary:	Yes he is. May I ask why you are calling?
You:	Yes, Linda, I am calling at the suggestion of Denise MacQueen. Denise and Mr. Jones know another through the Chamber of Commerce.
Secretary:	May I inquire into the nature of your call?
You:	Yes, I am contemplating a career change, and Denise felt Mr. Jones would be an excellent person to contact for some general advice and counsel.
Secretary:	I'm sorry, Ms. Johnson, but Mr. Jones does not provide job hunting assistance.
You:	I see, but I'm really not contacting him for a job. In fact, to the contrary, I wouldn't expect him to be aware of any job opportunities for me. What I do need, however, is some general advice and counsel. Denise said he is very knowledgeable of the chemical industry and might be willing to share some of his general insights and perspectives about what is happening in the industry. I would only need a few minutes of his time.
Secretary:	Well, generally he doesn't like to take this kind of call, but let me check.
You:	Thank you, Linda.

Note: Here again, you have attempted to shift the emphasis from "seeking a job" to seeking "general advice and counsel." People who avoid providing job-hunting advice are usually afraid that they will be asked for something they cannot deliver—a job. Rather than be embarrassed, they simply avoid such calls. By shifting the focus from a nondeliverable (a job) to a deliverable (advice and counsel), you remove the source of the embarrassment and enhance the probability that your call will be taken. Most people are quite willing to provide advice and counsel, and some will feel complimented that you have asked.

SCENARIO #6: (He's too busy, and won't be able to talk with you.)

Secretary:	Hello, Linda Robinson.
You:	Hello, this is Sally Johnson calling, Linda. Is Mr. Jones there please?
Secretary:	Yes. Does he know you?
You:	Yes, we met during the last Marketing Association meeting.
Secretary:	I see. May I ask why you are calling?
You:	Yes, I wanted to get some ideas and general thoughts about a career change I am contemplating. Because of his knowledge of the clothing industry, I felt he would be a good person to speak with.
Secretary:	Let me see if he can take your call.
You:	Thank you, Linda.
Secretary:	I'm sorry, Ms. Johnson, Mr. Jones has a very busy schedule and will not be able to talk with you.
You:	I see. I certainly don't want to bother him with this kind of request when he is busy. Would there be a better time to reach him? What does his schedule look like next week? When might be a good time for me to call back?
Secretary:	Let me check his schedule.
You:	Thank you.
Secretary:	Perhaps a good time to call would be next Thursday between 3:00 and 4:00 P.M. It's always hard to tell though. His schedule is so changeable.
You:	That's okay, Linda. I understand. Let me try

next Thursday at 3:00 P.M. Thank you for your help, Linda.

Secretary: You're quite welcome. Hope you reach him.

Note: The secretary's initial reply suggested that Jones may not want to speak with you at all, otherwise he would have offered to call back. A little polite assertiveness, however, had some payoff in this scenario. By offering to recall at a more convenient time, and asking the secretary's assistance in identifying a more convenient time to call, you have succeeded in breaking down the initial barrier and have been successful in winning the secretary over to your side.

SCENARIO #7: (Send him your resume, and he'll be glad to review it.)

Secretary: Hello, Mr. Jones' office.

You: Hello, with whom am I speaking, please?

Secretary: This is Linda Robinson.

You: Linda, this is Sally Johnson calling for Mr. Jones. Is he there?

Secretary: Yes, is he expecting your call, Sally?

You: No, but I was referred to him by my cousin, Craig Johnston. He and Craig are golfing buddies.

Secretary: Sally, may I ask why you are calling?

You: Yes, Craig tells me that Mr. Jones is very knowledgeable of the rubber industry, and he felt that Mr. Jones would be an excellent person to contact for some advice on a career move that I am considering.

Secretary: Oh, so you're looking for a job. Why don't you send him your resume, and I'm sure he would be pleased to review it.

You: That's an excellent idea; however, if his schedule permits, I would also appreciate the opportunity to talk with him as well. I really don't expect that he will be aware of specific jobs for me. What I really want to do, however, is to talk with him much more broadly about the rubber industry in general. I would also appreciate his general thoughts and ideas about my overall job search strategy. My cousin, Craig, says he has a lot of respect for Mr. Jones' general business knowledge. I will plan to send a copy of my resume as you suggested, Linda, but would there be a good time to plan to call him?

Secretary: Let me check his schedule.

You: Thank you.

Secretary: Why don't you try on Monday around 11:00 A.M. His schedule appears clear then, and he should be in his office.

You: Good, I will plan to call him then. In the meantime, I will send him a copy of my resume. Thanks for your help, Linda.

Secretary: You're very welcome.

Note: Although the secretary suggests that you send your resume to Jones for review, it's important that you let the secretary know that it is still important for you to speak directly with him. Simply sending your resume is not going to allow you to get the kind of information you are going to need from Jones to make your networking effort a success. Use the opportunity to emphasize this fact, and ask the secretary to help you to set up a convenient time for you to call back.

SCENARIO #8: (He has suggested you contact our employment department.)

Secretary: Hello, Mr. Jones' office. Linda Robinson speaking.

You:	Hello, Linda, this is Sally Johnson calling. Is Mr. Jones there, please?
Secretary:	Yes, he's in. Will he know you?
You:	No, but please let him know that I have been referred to him by Carolyn Beatty.
Secretary:	Ms. Johnson, what is this call in reference to?
You:	I am calling to seek his advice concerning a career change that I am making.
Secretary:	Okay, let me see if Mr. Jones can take your call.
You:	Thank you, Linda.
Secretary:	I spoke with Mr. Jones, and he suggests that you contact George Lawton, our employment manager.
You:	Fine, thank you, Linda, I will plan to do that. However, if at all possible, I would also like to talk to Mr. Jones when his schedule permits. Carolyn Beatty felt it might be beneficial for us to talk, since Mr. Jones is well-known in the recreation industry and could perhaps provide some helpful advice concerning my overall job search strategy. I would really appreciate his advice and counsel. Would there be a convenient time to call back?
Secretary:	I'll tell you what, let me ask him. I'll be right back to you in a moment, Ms. Johnson.
You:	Thank you, Linda.
Secretary:	I spoke with Mr. Jones, and he suggests that you call back about 2:00 P.M. today.
You:	Good. Thank you, Linda, I'll plan to call back at 2:00 P.M.

Note: Although initially rebuffed on your first attempt to reach your targeted contact, polite persistence can have excellent results. In this case favorable results were achieved by a more extensive explanation for why you needed to speak with Jones directly. Additionally, the restatement of the name of your referral, and reminder of this personal referral, creates a sense of personal obligation to take your call. It is difficult to ignore such personal referrals without incurring the potential for certain social risks.

Call Backs

Generally, if you have handled your initial calls with the secretary in a professional manner, there is a kind of dependency that develops. Once convinced that you have a legitimate need to talk with his/her boss, and there is a personal or professional obligation for the boss to respond, the secretary is "on your side." He or she transforms from the gatekeeper/protector (that is, one whose role is to protect the boss's time) to helper/facilitator (that is, one who is committed to bringing the two of you together). This makes return phone calls considerably easier.

Remember, in almost all cases you have asked the secretary for the best time to reach his or her boss, and have been given both a day and a specific time when the boss is expected to be there. If you should call and the boss is not there at the appointed hour, you will normally find the secretary a bit chagrined, with renewed and even stronger commitment to be of assistance to you. Your role, in such a case, is to be gracious and forgiving, but still committed to having direct conversation with the boss. Here is how such a conversation might go:

Secretary: Good morning, Linda Robinson speaking.
You: Good morning, Linda, this is Sally Johnson calling. I spoke to you last week, and you had suggested that this would be a good time to

KEYS TO EFFECTIVE RELATIONSHIP

	reach Mr. Jones to discuss my career plans. Is he in?
Secretary:	Oh yes, Sally, I do recall. Gee, I had really expected him to be in but, unfortunately, he was called out of the office unexpectedly. I'm sorry he's not here to take your call. Can I have him call you back?
You:	Yes, that would be just fine. When do you feel he might call?
Secretary:	He appears to have some time tomorrow morning. Let me see if I can get him to return your call then.
You:	That would be just great.
Secretary:	Fine. What is your phone number, Sally?
You:	My office number is 335-9284.
Secretary:	Thank you, Sally. I'll have him call you.
You:	I appreciate your help, Linda. Thank you.
Secretary:	You're very welcome.

Here is another variation of the same conversation:

Secretary:	Hello, Linda Robinson speaking.
You:	Hello, Linda. This is Sally Johnson calling for Mr. Jones. You may recall, I spoke with you last week and you had indicated that this might be a good time to reach Mr. Jones to discuss my anticipated career change.
Secretary:	Yes, Sally, I recall. Unfortunately, though, he's not here at the moment.
You:	I see. Well, that's too bad, I was looking forward to our discussion.
Secretary:	I'm sorry.
You:	That's alright, Linda. I understand. When do you feel I should call again?
Secretary:	Wednesday afternoon looks pretty good. You might try then.

You:	What time Wednesday afternoon would you suggest?
Secretary:	I think the safest would be between 4:00 and 5:00 P.M. He usually doesn't schedule any meetings after 4:00 P.M.
You:	Good. I'll try again on Wednesday at 4:00 P.M. Thank you, Linda.
Secretary:	You're welcome, Sally.

Review of these two mini dialogues will show that there are 4 common elements contained in each. These are:

1. A reminder of your previous call

2. A reminder of the reason for your call

3. A reminder that this was the time that the secretary had suggested that you call

4. The establishment of a specific day and time for follow-up (that is, your third call to the boss *or* the boss's return call to you)

You can "bet the ranch" that the secretary will really be embarrassed if his or her boss is not available the third time you place your call *or* if, after this second call, the boss neglects to return your call. In either event, should circumstances require a fourth call, you can also bet that the secretary will now feel an even stronger commitment to helping you. Sooner or later your effort and persistence will pay off, and you will be having direct dialogue with your targeted executive.

I think we have now pretty much succeeded in exhausting the subject of "getting through the secretary." In the next chapter we will be discussing the actual networking conversation itself.

CHAPTER

8

THE NETWORKING
PHONE CALL

W
e have already presented some overwhelming evidence of the importance of networking as the single most important job hunting technique. With some 70–80% of all professional, managerial, and executive positions filled through networking, why then would an intelligent, informed job seeker consciously choose not to use this as his or her primary job hunting tool? Good question!

Experience has shown that the two biggest deterrents to the use of employment networking are fear and embarrassment. These two emotions are commonly experienced by first-time networkers when contemplating use of the networking process for the very first time. So, if you have some concerns, you are not alone. You have plenty of company!

It is perfectly clear, however, that in order to effectively network, you will first need to overcome these emotions. Efficient networking will require that you are totally at ease with the mechanics of the networking process and that you feel upbeat and confident. Unless you deal positively with these emotions up front, at the beginning of your job search, you will find it most difficult to be effective at networking, and the likely result will be a greatly protracted job search.

It is certainly no easy matter to pick up the phone and call someone for help. This is especially true of something as personal and sensitive as a job search. We all have certain feelings of pride and independence. Being at the mercy of others, and needing to ask them for help and assistance, does not normally come easy to those who find themselves on the job market. These feelings of discomfort can be even further magnified for those who have been fired, rather than simply let go as part of an overall company downsizing.

No one disputes the existence of these negative feelings associated with the first initiation to the networking process. Such feelings are very real (and quite normal) for the vast majority who contemplate the use of this process. Nonetheless, unless you are fully prepared to wait a year or two to find employment, you had best deal with them right from the start! With some 70–80% (some say as high as 92%) of all jobs filled through networking (personal contact), it is simply not a process that you can afford to ignore!

So, let's take a look at both of these emotions—fear and embarrassment—from a more rational perspective. Perhaps by looking at them for what they "really are," we can "clear the deck" for a far more productive and successful job-hunting campaign.

OVERCOMING EMBARRASSMENT

Let's first address those feelings of embarrassment that begin to poke through when you first think about using networking as a job search method. It is likely that you will feel awkward and embarrassed when you think about asking friends and acquaintances for assistance in your job search. In some ways you may feel that this is demeaning. After all, most of us are proud and independent and have always been very self-sufficient. Additionally, you may feel awkward about the prospects of "taking advantage" of these special relationships. Asking for assistance in your job search is clearly a favor that transcends the more routine favors that you have likely felt comfortable asking of friends. All of these feelings are quite normal.

Well, let's examine this concept of "friendship." What is it all about? What does being a "friend" really mean? And, how does it relate to networking?

As we know, friends are much more than mere social acquaintances. Other than immediate family, friends are the only true support system that we have during those times in our lives when things are looking rather bleak. Friendship means much more than social companionship. It is a much deeper relationship that incorporates a sense of love and caring—one that includes an unspoken mutual commitment to protect and help one another without expectation of receiving anything in return. In fact, it is the very act of giving freely to one another, without expectations, that reaffirms and strengthens the bonds of this special relationship.

Certainly, asking for some help on your job search from a friend will hardly be stressful to your relationship. On the contrary, you will find that most friends will do "all they can" to be of help to you. Most, in fact, will feel good that you feel comfortable enough with your relationship to turn to them in your time of need.

Although there may not be quite the same depth of relationship with acquaintances as you experience with close friends, you will nonetheless find that the great majority of acquaintances will also be more than happy to assist you with your job search. With all of the corporate downsizing that is taking place in America, most have already been personally touched in some way by unemployment. Chances are these very same acquaintances, who you plan to contact, have had family, friends, or other acquaintances who have been laid off. Or, they may have personally tasted the sharpness of the corporate downsizing cleaver. Others will quickly identify with your plight, feeling that "There, but for the grace of God, go I."

There is no longer the stigma attached to being unemployed that there was several years ago. At one time, when jobs were plentiful and employers were not cutting back for competitive reasons, being unemployed suggested that you were lazy, shiftless, or incompetent. This is no longer true. Today, with all the corporate downsizing and layoffs, it is widely known that many have been affected through absolutely no fault of their own. It is simply a "numbers game," and there are some awfully talented persons out there who simply happened to be at the wrong place at the wrong time.

Thus, today, there is nothing to be ashamed of if you find yourself among the ranks of the unemployed. You have plenty of good company! This just happens to be a temporary condition that, with a good game plan and a little help from others, will pass, and you will return to the more comfortable role of contributor and provider. Clearly, there is no need for embarrassment.

If you are still experiencing some reservations about asking others for help in your job search, let me provide some further evidence of people's willingness to help others. Consider, for the moment, that it is not uncommon for persons to risk their very lives by diving into icy waters or entering a burning building for the purpose of rescuing complete strangers. What motivates people to do this? The answer is fairly simple. Most people really do care about others. Most have a natural, intrinsic drive to help others in a time of need. It is what they would expect of others, should they find themselves in similar circumstances.

Clearly, if people didn't want to help others, the employment networking process wouldn't work. Yet, millions of job seekers have successfully used networking to land their jobs, time and time again! The fact that 70–80% of all jobs are filled through some form of networking provides some awfully strong evidence of the willingness of others to help out.

Finally, if I still haven't convinced you of people's willingness to help you with your job search, let me try one more time. Let's try the networking process in reverse. How would you feel if you received the following call?

> Hello, Dick, this is Karl Swanson calling. I am a friend of John Thomson (a close friend of yours) and have heard John speak of you several times. It's too bad we haven't met personally, but I know we've come very close on several occasions. I suppose one of these days our schedules will mesh.
>
> Dick, during a recent conversation with John about my current job search, he suggested that I contact you, feeling that perhaps you might be in a position to lend me a hand. Don't get me wrong, Dick, I certainly don't expect that you will be aware of specific job opportunities for me. What I'm really looking for is some general advice and ideas concerning my job-hunting strategy. John tells me that you are very knowledgeable about the food industry, and would be a good person to talk with. Is this a convenient time for you?

Well, how about it? How do you feel about this kind of approach? Under the circumstances, would you be willing to spend a few minutes to help Karl with his job search? Chances are you would be. After all, Karl has been referred to you by a close friend, who you both know, and his request is hardly unreasonable. Well, the point is, if you are willing to lend Karl a hand, chances are there are hundreds of others out there who would be just as willing to help you, if approached in a similar manner. Millions of others, who have used networking to find employment, have already proven this to be true.

DEALING WITH FEAR

Now, let's tackle that remaining emotional barrier to effective networking—fear!

It is common to feel more than a little anxiety the first time that you pick up that telephone to make a networking call. I have seen many a veteran, seasoned executive who, under normal circumstances is brimming with confidence, go "rubber kneed" on that first call or two. So, if it is any solace, you are not alone. If you are feeling a little anxious about this process, you have plenty of good company. Calling others on the phone to ask for job-hunting assistance is hardly something that one does as part of his or her daily routine. For most, it does not come naturally and will, therefore, require a little adjusting.

It is believed that the fear associated with employment networking can generally be classified into two categories as follows:

• Fear of the unknown (not knowing what to expect)

• Fear of rejection (others will refuse to help you)

If approached rationally, these fears can easily be overcome, and you can be on your way to a highly successful networking effort and bright, rewarding career. Let's look at these two kinds of fear a little more closely.

With respect to employment networking, fear of the unknown is believed to be caused by the networker's lack of experience with the networking process. He or she simply does not know what to expect.

It is believed that there is a high degree of correlation between this kind of fear and the networker's preparedness. If the networker is ill-prepared, and has not practiced his or her networking approach prior to the first call, the fear associated with networking is likely to be high. Conversely, if the networker is well-prepared and has thoroughly practiced his or her networking approach prior to this first call, the fear of networking is considerably reduced and the networker feels more comfortable.

Thus, one key to controlling the fear of networking is through preparation and rehearsal. If you have steadfastly developed a good networking script as the basis for your discussions, anticipated and prepared responses for the most likely questions you will encounter, and had plenty of mock rehearsals, you will have successfully allayed the majority of your pre-networking jitters and will be prepared to launch a highly productive networking campaign.

Fear of rejection, on the other hand, is also a powerful inhibitor to executing a successful networking process. However, as with fear of the unknown, it has little basis.

As discussed earlier in this chapter, the vast majority of persons you contact through networking will be more than willing to be of assistance to you in your job search. I would place the number at about 97% , with 3% (or less) abstaining. Thus, you are knowingly starting with a 97% probable success rate—a pretty impressive statistic! The sheer fact that 70–80% of all jobs are filled through the use of networking (personal contact) should also provide some very convincing evidence that a high percentage of people will provide job-hunting assistance, if asked.

As an experienced executive search consultant, I have had considerable, first-hand networking experience and have literally made thousands of telephone calls to others asking them for assistance. In my case, instead of looking for job leads, as is done in employment networking, I am looking for the names of qualified candidates to fill professional or managerial positions with my clients. This is not dissimilar to employment networking, where one of your key goals is to ask for the names of persons who may be able to help you identify job opportunities. In both cases we are requesting the names of "key contacts," who may be in a position to help us.

In all of the thousands of networking calls (we call them "sourcing calls" in executive search business) that I have made over the last 7 years, the number of calls where persons *flatly* refused to help can be counted on one hand. This is not to say that there weren't other calls where individuals couldn't think of appropriate contacts. This occurs more frequently. The point is, however, when making networking or sourcing calls, if you use a reasonable approach, the number of outright "rejections" is exceedingly small.

Outright rejection (refusal to help) is particularly rare when the networking contact has been made through personal referral. The vast majority of persons will honor such personal introductions and offer to be of help to you. On straight "cold calls" (calls in which there is no personal association or introduction), however, the number of rejections will increase somewhat. (This is to be expected, since there is no longer a sense of personal or professional obligation to respond.) In any event, whether a personal referral or cold call, if the networking process is well-planned and -executed, the number of outright rejections will be unusually small and should not hamper your job-hunting efforts in any way.

Nonetheless, you must be mentally prepared for a few outright rejections along the way. Unfortunately, few as these may be, there are still going to be a handful of persons who will refuse to help you in any way. Don't take these rejections personally. They are normal and should be fully expected as a natural part of the networking process. Where you run into such persons, simply thank them for taking your call and quickly move on to your next call. This handful of narrowly focused, self-centered persons is simply not worth your time or concern. So don't dwell on them.

For positive motivation, when you encounter one of these rejections, it is good to remember the advice offered by many seasoned outplacement consultants. Every "no" you get is one step closer to a "yes." So don't take these "no's" personally, and move on to your next contact. A "yes" is just around the corner.

As I have shown, there is no excuse for letting either fear or embarrassement get in the way of your employment networking efforts. Experience has shown that outright rejection is rare, so there is little basis for this fear. Secondly, with a good networking script and a little practice, you can replace pre-networking anxiety with a confident, positive attitude. So let's now move on to helping you prepare for a positive and effective networking experience.

THE NETWORKING CONCEPT

In order to understand why the networking process has historically proven such a powerful job-hunting concept, it is important to understand the underlying principles that are responsible for its success. Let's take a few moments here to examine these.

First, networking is an exponential process. What is meant by "exponential" is that the process enables you to take a base of direct personal contacts (which you personally have) and multiply these contacts substantially through the process of networking through others.

For those of you who have had a course in biology and understand the theory of cell division, by which all living organisms grow, the mathematical progression of networking is easy to understand. From a graphical standpoint, it looks like this:

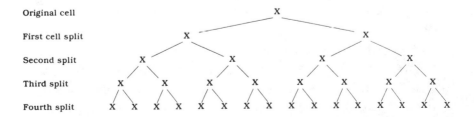

The original cell splits, forming two cells. Each of these cells splits into two cells, forming a total of 4 cells. These 4 cells now split into two cells each, for a total of 8 cells. Finally, in our illustration, these 8 cells each split into two cells, for a grand total of 16 cells.

The mathematical progression of networking works very similarly to that of cell division. The original cell is you. By calling just 2 friends and asking them to each refer you to 2 of their friends, you have expanded your network of contacts to 4 persons. By asking each of these 4 persons to refer you to 2 of their friends or acquaintances, your network of contacts has expanded to 8. By obtaining the names of 2 additional referrals from each of these 8, the mathematical progression continues and your total network has now expanded to a grand total of 16 persons. If this process continues, it would be quite possible to geometrically expand your pool of contacts to several hundred persons within a fairly short period of time.

Thus, like cell division, the networking process allows you to substantially expand a small group of personal, direct contacts to a very sizable group of contacts, all of which become active (at various levels of participation) in helping you with your job search. This has the cumulative effect of considerably multiplying your job search efforts, thus substantially increasing the probability of a successful result.

The theory of employment networking goes on to say that by continuously expanding your networking contacts, sooner or later these contacts will lead to personal introductions at companies that you have targeted for employment purposes. By continuing to network, using the expanding contacts you develop within each of these target companies, sooner or later you will end up with a personal introduction to your targeted executive (that is, the person who has the power—and hopefully the need—to hire you).

The second underlying principle that is believed to account for the power of the networking process as a job search method is the "sense of obligation" that it creates.

Since each networking contact you make has been brought about by "personal referral" (you have been referred by someone who that person knows), the networkee generally feels a sense of personal or professional obligation to assist you. To do otherwise could be construed as a personal or professional affront to the person who has made the referral.

Certainly, it stands to reason that you are in a far more powerful position to make something happen when, during your introduction, you can say to the networkee, "John Smith (a personal friend or business associate of the networkee) suggested you might be a good person to talk with" versus "I understand that you are the Director of Marketing at Arlington Corporation." The fact that you know John Smith, and have been referred by him, automatically creates a certain personal bond and a sense of personal obligation that could never be realized through a cold call into the company.

There is also a strong preference for managers to hire persons who are known to them, rather than to hire complete strangers. Other employment sources such as employment advertising, search firms, and employment agencies, generally yield candidates who are not known by the hiring manager or other members of this manager's firm. In such cases, the hiring manager must rely upon interviewing skills and the opinions of outside references to gauge the qualifications and fit of these strangers. Most managers perceive this more risky than when the candidate is referred by another firm member, who can personally vouch for the candidate's traits, qualifications, work ethic, and the like.

So this unique combination of increasing mathematical expansion of your networking base of contacts, coupled with the sense of personal obligation and credibility created by the networking process, makes employment networking the most effective job hunting technique by far. No other employment source or technique can even come close!

THE "HIDDEN JOB MARKET" CONCEPT

Knowledgeable employment authorities have long believed that a substantial percentage (most frequently estimated at 80%) of jobs never become known to the general public. These positions comprise what is commonly known as the "hidden job market" and are filled (through personal contact) long before they have the opportunity to become known to the public through such sources as newspaper advertising, executive search firms, employment agencies, and other such traditional job-hunting sources. Thus, only an estimated 20% of all job openings ever become known to the public.

If you restrict your job search to only these conventional public sources (newspaper ads, search firms, employment agencies, and so on), you severely hamper your job-hunting efforts. By doing so, you are concentrating your efforts on those sources that are known to produce only 20% of the results. By extending your efforts to include employment networking, however, you suddenly include the remaining 80% of the market, thus substantially increasing the probabilities for a successful job search.

The key to the hidden job market is, of course, employment networking. By developing and continuously expanding your network of contacts and referrals, you will begin to penetrate the hidden job market and discover jobs of which others are unaware.

Another interesting statistic that you should keep in mind when contemplating the importance of employment networking is that some 43.8% of the jobs that are filled through networking are *newly created*. This means that these positions did not formally exist prior to the personal contact being made, and they were created specifically for the candidate. This data is courtesy of Harvard sociologist, Dr. Mark S. Granovetter, who conducted an extensive study concerning how people find jobs. Granovetter's work makes it clear that networking can have some really direct pay-off as far as your job hunting campaign is concerned (see Chapter 2).

Employment networking can also provide you with some very real competitive advantage by reducing your competition or even eliminating it entirely. Since such networking allows you to assess the hidden job market and pursue opportunities that have not become known to the general public, it should stand to reason that there will be less competition. By contrast, jobs that have become known to the general public through such sources as recruitment advertising, employment agencies, and the like will attract far more candidates, and the competition may be intense.

It should be quite evident that there is considerable value to be gained by utilizing employment networking as your primary job-hunting technique. Without it, you have effectively eliminated 80% of the job market and substantially increased your competition. With it, you have expanded your search to include the lion's share (80%) of the market and substantially reduced the intensity of the competition. Surely it should stand to reason that if some 70–80% of all professional and managerial positions are filled through this process, you cannot afford to ignore the importance of this job hunting technique. It should likely comprise some 70–80% of your job search time and effort.

NETWORKING OBJECTIVE

Although the ultimate objectives of the employment networking process is to secure interviews and job offers, these are truly more the "end results" of a good networking process rather than the immediate "objectives" of such a process.

The immediate objectives of employment networking will vary depending upon the person you are contacting and his or her ability to help. These shorter-term objectives include the following:

1. Secure names of key contacts

2. Secure introductions to key contacts

3. Secure information (target industries/companies)

4. Secure job-hunting advice

5. Secure job leads

Although possible, it is unlikely that a close personal friend (unless working in a related industry or occupation) will be able to produce direct job leads, names of key target industry contacts, or specific target industry information. Usually, at best, these friends will be able to provide you with general business and personal contacts, and some general advice concerning your job hunting campaign, resume, and so on.

By contrast, a target industry trade association executive is far more likely to know of specific job leads, names of key target industry contacts, and key information about companies in the industry (expansions, contractions, and so on). Likewise, if you work in a generic service function (accounting, human resources, procurement, or the like), a professional association executive (or member) is more apt to be aware of specific openings in your field. Such persons, however, are less likely than trade association executives to be aware of specific opportunities or developments within your target industries.

Thus, when utilizing the networking process, the objective of each networking contact will need to be altered to fit the circumstances if you are to maximize the results of these important contacts. Before making each networking call, therefore, it will be important to set some specific objectives and to modify your approach to fit the particular circumstances.

THE PRIMARY (LEVEL I) CONTACT LIST

The first step in preparing for networking is to prepare a comprehensive list of people you know. According to employment and outplacement authorities, this list should include the names of everyone you can think of, regardless of whether or not you believe they can be of help to you in your job search. This list should include at least 100 to 200 persons.

The following classifications are provided to assist you in preparing this Level I contact list, and will hopefully serve to jog your memory regarding persons whose names may not immediately come to mind.

Social Contacts

Friends	Relatives
Neighbors	Acquaintances
Social club officers	Social club members
Church members	

Educational Contacts

Teachers	School administration
Professors	Alumni association officers
Class officers	Fraternity members
Fellow alumni	Sorority members
Class members	Placement office administration

Community Contacts

Public office holders	Politicians
Service club officers	Service club members
Business leaders	Bank officers
Public accountants	Attorneys
Business brokers	Stock brokers
Insurance agents	Chamber of Commerce
Clergy	Doctor
Dentist	Barber
Beautician	Store owners

Business Contacts

Industry leaders
Competitors
Salespersons
Consultants
Headhunters
Vendors/suppliers
Customers
Past employers
Insurance agents
Bank officers
Attorneys
Business brokers

Trade association officers
Trade association members
Professional association
  officers
Professional association
  members
Bosses (current/past)
Co-workers (current/past)
Subordinates (current/past)
Public accountants
Venture capitalists
Stock brokers

PRIORITIZATION OF PRIMARY CONTACTS

Having completed your list of primary contacts, it is now important to prioritize them according to their relevance to your job search. It is suggested that you prioritize them using the following classifications:

Priority #1. Those individuals from your target companies who would likely have an interest in your background and who have the power to hire you.

Priority #2. Those persons who are most likely to be aware of job opportunities in your target companies and could provide valuable introductions.

Priority #3. Those individuals who are knowledgeable of your target industries and have key contacts.

Priority #4. Those who may have contacts in your target industries.

Priority #5. Friends, acquaintances, and others who are unlikely to have contacts in your key target industries, but have good business contacts.

Priority #6. All others.

By prioritizing your list of 100 to 200 primary Level I contacts in this fashion, you are selecting those that are most relevant to your job search objectives. Primary focus is on those who are most likely able to provide you with meaningful information and contacts. This will enable you to shortcut the process somewhat by cutting down on the total number of contacts you will need to make prior to landing employment interviews and job offers. Considering the size of your primary contacts list (100 to 200 persons), this prioritization, if carefully applied, could cut several months off the time necessary to successfully conclude your job search.

One key mistake that job hunters frequently make is to start by networking with close friends and acquaintances. Although this provides a certain comfort level, many of these may be least able to provide you with the valuable contacts and introductions you will need to land job interviews with your target companies. Instead, you need to focus your calls on those top priority contacts who have the highest probability of being able to provide you with meaningful assistance.

Perhaps a half-dozen or so "warm up" calls to close friends at the very beginning of the networking effort may be a good idea. This will enable you to work out the kinks in your networking approach, and add some refinements before moving on to more valuable contacts. As soon as you are feeling comfortable with the networking process, however, you are best advised to move on to higher priority contacts, who can meaningfully impact your job search. To do so will likely cut valuable time from both your networking and overall job search process. Little can be gained from continuing to focus on low priority contacts, except to waste valuable time and substantially protract the job search process.

KEY ELEMENTS OF THE NETWORKING CALL

Careful analysis of the employment networking process will reveal that the following basic elements are present in most successful employment networking calls:

1. Introduction
2. Name and Relationship of Referral
3. Small Talk
4. Purpose of Your Call
5. Reason for Your Availability (Optional)
6. Summary of Your Background (The 2-Minute Drill)
7. Specific Requests for Assistance
    a. Request for Personal Meeting
    b. Request for General Information & Advice
    c. Request for Names of Key Contacts
    d. Request to Use Name as a Referral
8. "Thank You" for Assistance

We will now spend some time discussing each of these key elements, so that you might better appreciate the role each plays in an effective employment networking call.

INTRODUCTION

The introduction of the employment networking call is pretty basic, and is similar to that used in any good business call. It consists of a salutation, followed by introduction of the caller by name. The following are some sample introductions:

> Good morning, Mr. Wheaton. This is Steve Davidson calling. How are you this morning?

> Hello, Jane. This is David Johnson calling.
>
> Good afternoon, Dick. This is Carolyn Smythe. How are you this afternoon?

The specific salutation used during the introduction to most employment networking calls normally includes the typical fare of "Good morning," "Good afternoon," "Good evening," or simply "Hello." There are no particular rules that seem to govern which of these is chosen.

There are some simple rules, however, which govern how you should address the individual you are calling.

1. Unless you are friends or acquaintances who are already on a first-name basis, never address the recipient of your call by a first name (or nickname) if they answer the phone using the personal title "Mr.," "Mrs.," or "Ms." Such persons tend to be more formal and may resent it if you were to call them by a first name, without their expressed permission.

2. Even though a person may answer the phone using a first (or nickname)followed by their last name, don't automatically assume that this is a free license to address them informally by their first name. If the person is considerably older than you, or if his or her job level is substantially higher than yours, it is probably wise to show appropriate respect by addressing them with the appropriate personal title ("Mr.," "Mrs.," or "Ms.").

3. Where there is no reasonable age difference or job level differential, and the persons whom you are calling answer the phone by their first names (or nicknames) followed by last names, you should feel free to address them by their first names. In fact, this is preferred since such informality is conducive to establishing a closer personal bond which can prove helpful to your networking objectives.

4. In the case of close friends and acquaintances (or close friends of same), you are strongly encouraged to use first names (or nicknames) wherever possible. Again, this tends to strengthen the personal bond and create a stronger sense of personal relationship that will likely prove additive to your networking efforts.

In all cases you should use your first name (or nickname) followed by your last name, when introducing yourself. This encourages an informal, friendlier conversation and places your target "networkee" more at ease.

Although a dwindling custom in modern day business telephone conversations, it is still not uncommon to inquire about another's general health and overall well-being by saying something like, "How are you this morning?" This show of personal concern can likewise add a note of personal interest that can help to set the stage for friendlier conversation.

NAME AND RELATIONSHIP OF REFERRAL

Following the introduction, it is important to state the name of your referral and to describe the nature of your relationship. This helps to cement the personal bond that is so important to successful networking. The following are offered as brief examples:

> Mr. Johnson, Barbara Matthews suggested I give you a call. Barbara and I were formerly neighbors in Newport Beach.

> Joe, I was referred to you by Steve Temple. Steve is a tennis buddy of mine.

> Ms. Turner, Fred Arnold suggested that you would be a good person for me to contact. Fred and I attended Bucknell University together and were fraternity brothers.

As you can see from these examples, both the name of your referral and the nature of your relationship are fully described. This serves to establish a sense of personal connection and bonding that will normally prove quite helpful in improving the overall effectiveness of the employment networking process.

SMALL TALK

The purpose of small talk is to create a warmer, friendlier atmosphere that will help to set the stage for the networking conversation to come. It also begins to draw the "networkee" into the conversation in a way that is informal and non-threatening, establishing a more congenial atmosphere as the basis for the discussion.

The following examples of small talk should serve to give you some ideas about how to get started.

You:	Steve tells me that you're quite a tennis player. He says that you have one of the strongest serves that he's ever had to face.
Networkee:	He should talk. Have you ever seen his backhand?
You:	Yeah, it's pretty strong.
Networkee:	Darn right! He has a mean cross court shot.
You:	Sally said to say "hello" to you. She and I worked together in Human Resources at the Clarke Company.
Networkee:	Really? Gee, I haven't seen Sally for at least five years. How is she doing?
You:	Just great! She was recently promoted to Vice President of Human Resources at MacCain Corporation.

Networkee:	No kidding? She was always a hard worker. I always thought she'd rise to the top. That's great news!
You:	Dave Lord and I know one another from the American Manufacturer's Association. We have had dinner several times together. He's quite an interesting guy.
Networkee:	Yes, I have a lot of respect for Dave's knowledge of manufacturing systems.
You:	Yes, he sure is knowledgeable in the systems area. I understand that he's particularly knowledgeable of MRP applications.
Networkee:	I wouldn't be surprised.

As you can see from the foregoing sample dialogues, small talk can be used quite effectively to strengthen the personal connection between you and the networkee. Additionally, it serves to provide a smooth transition between the introduction and the beginning of the actual networking discussion. This more personalized atmosphere should facilitate a more effective and productive discussion between the two of you and better help you to realize your employment networking objectives.

PURPOSE OF YOUR CALL

The important rule to remember when stating the reason for your call is *never ask for a job*! To do so will immediately put people off, and they will begin to recoil and adapt a defensive stance. This is not the way you want to get your networking conversation started.

By asking for a job or strongly implying that the networkee can help you to find one, at this stage of the conversation, creates an unrealistic expectation against which the networkee may well not be able to deliver. This tends to place the networkee on the spot, causing him or her to feel uncomfortable. Additionally, such a direct approach suggests that you lack sensitivity or class, and may be viewed by many networkees as bold, forward, or offensive.

Why do this to the networkee just at the point in the conversation when your immediate objective should be to put the person at ease and to establish personal rapport? At this stage in the conversation your purpose should be to gain their general support and to enlist their desire to assist you in your overall job search effort. It is not to simply "help you find a job."

Most experts agree that the best approach to use at this stage of the conversation is a more indirect or oblique one. Instead of asking them for assistance in finding a job, tell them that you are calling for *information* and *advice* concerning your job search.

The important thing to remember here is that, although most persons with whom you talk will not be aware of a specific job opportunity for you, practically all are in a position to offer you some kind of information and/or advice. You are thus asking them for something they can deliver. This avoids the unnecessary embarrassment and awkwardness that can result when they are asked for something which they cannot provide (jobs, job leads). Rest assured, if they are aware of specific opportunities for which you are qualified, they will volunteer this information during the course of your discussion.

Here are some examples of how you might introduce the purpose of your call:

You: John, I am in the process of leaving my position as Controller of Warner Cable, and Bob seemed to feel that you might be a good person to talk with concerning the general state of the cable TV industry. He says that you are very knowledgeable guy and tend to have some creative ideas. I would welcome any thoughts or suggestions you might have concerning the industry and/or my overall job search strategy.

You: Ms. Langford, I have decided to make a career change, and Jim seemed to feel you would be a good person to speak with. As President of the Food Marketing Association, he thought you would be in an excellent position to share some broad observations about the industry and to perhaps suggest key persons with whom I should be in contact.

You: George, I will be leaving my position as Manager of Technology at Velstar Corporation and Peggy seemed to feel that you might be a good person to contact. She tells me that you are Technology Director at Wellkraft and may be in a position to offer some general advice and ideas concerning my career change. I would certainly welcome your thoughts and suggestions.

You: Mr. Porter, I have recently left my position as Vice President of Manufacturing at Random Corporation and am seeking a new career opportunity. As President of one of Random's major competitors, and as a key leader in the electronic industry, I felt you would be an excellent person to talk with concerning current developments in our industry. I would also appreciate any general thoughts or advice you might offer concerning my overall job search strategy.

You will note that in the preceding mini dialogues there is no mention of the words "job" or "job leads." Instead, the focus is on securing advice, information, suggestions, thoughts, observations, and ideas.

This kind of indirect approach will go a long way toward establishing good rapport and encouraging a far more productive conversation. You are asking networkees for something they can deliver, and you are avoiding putting them on the spot by asking them for something they cannot or don't want to deliver (jobs and job leads) at this early stage of the networking discussion. As the conversation warms up and the networkee begins to feel more comfortable with you and your background, however, the conversation may well lead to discussion of specific job opportunities. The point is, however, don't try to force this conversation prematurely or you may jeopardize an excellent opportunity to pick up some meaningful information.

One other observation needs to be made concerning the approach used in the preceding mini dialogues, which should prove helpful to your effectiveness as a networker. You will note that, where possible, there has been an additional reference to the person who has referred you to the networkee. This helps to create a closer feeling of personal bonding and a greater sense of obligation to respond on the part of the networkee. It is, of course, not possible to achieve this when the networking call is a "cold call," with no actual referral having been made.

REASON FOR YOUR AVAILABILITY (OPTIONAL)

Generally, it is unnecessary for you to volunteer a specific reason for your availability. As in the preceeding sample dialogues, it is quite sufficient to say that you are "in the process of making a career change" or that you "have decided to leave General Electric." It is certainly not necessary to offer this information to the networkee, unless you are asked to do so.

Volunteering such information up front may, in fact, have a negative impact on your networking discussion. This is particularly true if you were let go by your employer for what are perceived to be negative reasons (poor performance, insubordination, inappropriate behavior, and so on). Even being let go as part of a general downsizing may create premature suspicion on the part of the networkee. Why were you let go rather than someone else? Why was your position eliminated rather than another one? These are some of the questions that may tend to creep into the networkee's mind. The resultant suspicion may cause the networkee to feel reluctant ánd cause him or her to withhold certain information and/or contacts that might have proven very worthwhile to your job search. Why take this chance?

My general recommendation is to avoid volunteering the specific reasons for your availability. Just stating that you are available is sufficient. Don't volunteer reasons unless you are asked.

For those of you who have been let go as a part of a corporate downsizing or job elimination, if you feel compelled to volunteer a reason, keep it short and sweet. If you absolutely feel you must, then let me suggest the following ways of phrasing this statement:

You: I am leaving my position as Manager of Procurement at Power Corporation as a result of a corporate downsizing, and I am seeking other opportunities in the materials management field.

You: My position as Corporate Employment Manager at Reardon Company has been eliminated, and I am now seeking other opportunities in the employment or human resources field.

By no means should you volunteer the reason for your availability if it is for negative reasons. The employment networking process is not the time for true confessions. Save your explanations for the appropriate moment during the employment interview, but don't destroy your chances of getting good leads and contacts before your employment campaign has even had a chance to get off the ground.

SUMMARY OF YOUR BACKGROUND (THE 2-MINUTE DRILL)

At the appropriate point during the employment networking discussion, you will likely need to provide the networkee with a short summary of your background and qualifications. In some job-hunting and outplacement quarters, this is sometimes referred to as the "2-minute drill." This name derives from the popularly held belief that you need to be prepared to present a brief, succinct biographical sketch that effectively communicates your job objective, experience, and key strengths and abilities to the networkee in a span of 2 minutes or less.

Frequently you will have the opportunity to deliver your 2-minute summary shortly following the statement describing the purpose of your call. It is typically at this point that the networkee will make a brief inquiry concerning your background and qualifications. Like a 2-minute commercial, this biographical presentation must do an effective job of marketing your qualifications as well as leaving a memorable impression with the networkee.

Since you will frequently need to deliver this verbal summary numerous times during the networking process, and the content and delivery of this presentation will have a major impact on the effectiveness and outcome of your networking efforts, you would be well-advised to practice this presentation at length. In fact, I strongly recommend that you start by preparing a finely tuned script as the basis for this 2-minute drill. You should then rehearse this script several times, until you are thoroughly familiar with it and can automatically recite it at a moment's notice.

Since there is such a wide range of experiences and backgrounds, it is difficult to develop a universal script that will fit all persons. The following sample scripts, however, should serve to give you the right idea.

You: Michael, I have over 15 years of employment experience. Most recently I was Manager of Corporate Employment for Ogdon Corporation, a *Fortune* 300 consumer products company, where I managed a staff of 6 and was responsible for all corporate staff recruiting. I also provided employment support to the company's 4 manufacturing divisions. Prior experience includes Manager of Technical Employment for Ogdon, 3 years as Administrative Employment Manager with Drissel Corporation, a $200 million manufacturer of electric tools; and nearly 6 years as an employment professional with Messier Company, a small consulting firm providing consulting services to the electrical and electronics industry. I have strong management recruiting and selection skills and am known for my ability to effectively manage a high volume employment department. I am looking for a challenging management position in the corporate employment department of a major corporation or as Director of Employment in a smaller organization.

You: I am a young, ambitious accounting professional with 4 years of experience, and am looking for my first supervisory or management experience. I hold an M.A. in Business, with an Accounting emphasis, and have 4 years experience with Dexter Corporation, where I advanced from Accountant to Cost Accountant to Senior Cost Accountant. I have a strong background in both cost and general accounting, and have enjoyed a good reputation as a strong producer. I particularly enjoy manufacturing cost accounting, and am seeking a position as a manager or supervisor in the cost accounting field.

You: I am a sales management professional with over 6 years of experience in successfully selling complex business systems requiring exceptional application sales skills. I have demonstrated the ability to successfully introduce new, high-ticket business systems product lines involving complex business and institutional applications. Most recently, I was District Sales Manager for the Detroit Regional Office of Micro Graphics, Inc., a $500 million manufacturer of microfilm storage and retrieval systems. My district introduced the new Z-Line retrieval system a full 6 months later than any other sales district, and by year-end our sales were double that of the next best district. I have been with Micro Graphics for 5 years, and have advanced through the positions of Sales Representative, Senior Sales Representative to my current position as District Manager. I am a 1986 graduate of the University of Michigan with a degree in marketing, and I am looking for a position as Regional or National Sales Manager with a major manufacturer of business systems.

As you can see from these examples, the presentation of your biographical summary needs to be short, sweet, and to the point. In each case it provides a brief description of your overall background—your current and past positions. A brief attempt is also made to highlight some of your key strengths and accomplishments, and a statement of your job objective is provided as well. This thumbnail sketch is designed to provide the networkee with just enough background to understand your credentials and objectives, but is not so detailed as to be overwhelming and cause an information overload.

SPECIFIC REQUESTS FOR ASSISTANCE

As previously mentioned in this chapter, you should have a specific objective in mind when placing your networking call. In each case, you will be asking for specific assistance from the networkee. Whether requesting a personal meeting, general information and/or advice, names of key contacts, or permission to use the networkee's name as a referral, you will need the networkee's help in moving your job search forward to a successful conclusion.

Request for Personal Meeting

Where you have reason to believe that the individual you are calling has key target industry contacts, your primary objective should be to arrange for a personal meeting between the two of you. Such a meeting is commonly referred to in the outplacement trade as an "informational interview;" however, you should refrain from calling it such during discussion with the networkee. Also, in requesting this meeting, you will want to avoid any discussion of your background. Thus, there is no need for you to go into your 2-minute drill during this preliminary conversation. Instead, after having established the purpose of your call, simply request a personal meeting with the networkee.

There is clear evidence that a personal, face-to-face meeting can be a very powerful tool in getting others committed to helping you with your job search. One well-known Chicago-based outplacement consulting firm really pushes the face-to-face informational interview as a critical technique in the job search process. This firm states that 92% of all clients they counsel find positions through employment networking. Further, its clients successfully conclude their job searches in an average 3.2 months compared to the out-placement consulting industry average of about 5 months. This firm has thus presented some fairly convincing evidence supporting the effectiveness of the informational interview that cannot be ignored.

In my opinion, however, there is the danger of wasting considerable time meeting with persons who are not likely to have contacts in the industries or companies that you have targeted for your job search. Good common sense should prevail here, so that you make productive use of your time. Obviously, many more persons can be contacted by phone than in person. So choose your targets for informational interview meetings carefully and make sure that you are not using valuable time to have personal meetings with those who cannot help your cause.

The following should prove helpful in illustrating how you might go about requesting the opportunity for an informational interview:

You: Bob, I have decided to leave my position as Manager of Procurement at Drake Chemical Company to seek a position offering greater career growth prospects. George tells me that you have an excellent knowledge of the specialty chemicals industry and would be a good person to talk with concerning my career plans. I would enjoy stopping by to see you for 30 minutes or so to discuss my career plans and to get your overall ideas and suggestions. If you are agreeable, when would be a convenient time for you to meet with me?

You: Ms. Patterson, I am in the process of a career change and will be seeking a senior level position in corporate planning. Dave Kennedy tells me that you are an officer in the American Planning Society and would be an excellent person to talk with to get an overview of current developments in the planning field. I was wondering whether you would be kind enough to meet with me for a half-hour or so to share some of your observations about the field as well as general suggestions concerning my career plans.

You: Linda, Karl Swanson suggested I give you a call. I am making a career change and will be looking for a management position in the public affairs field. Karl says that you have worked in the field of public affairs for several years and have a lot of contacts. Would it be possible for us to meet for a half-hour or so? I would really appreciate the opportunity to discuss my career plans with you, and would welcome any ideas and suggestions you might have to offer concerning my overall job search strategy.

You will note in these examples that the caller studiously avoids directly asking the networkee for assistance in finding a job. Instead, the approach is a fairly soft, indirect one. Reasons stated for requesting this meeting are such things as:

- To discuss overall career plans
- To get overall ideas and suggestions on your job search strategy
- To secure observations and information on developments and trends in a given field or industry that could impact your job search
- To get general advice and counsel on a career transition you are currently considering

This indirect approach is intended to avoid putting the networkee on the spot. The request for "advice," "counsel," "suggestions," "ideas," observations," and so on is reasonable and is something that the networkee can actually deliver. Some, in fact, will consider your request as a compliment since you obviously value their opinion on the subject.

REQUEST FOR INFORMATION AND ADVICE

Where a face-to-face meeting is not a practical consideration, you may wish to ask the networkee for information and advice as an alternate strategy. This is again a far more acceptable approach than directly asking for assistance in finding a job.

Requests for information and advice can fall into several categories. Some key ones are as follows:

career plans

job-hunting strategies

industry developments

Here are some examples of how you might use the networking call to secure information and advice.

You: Mary, Steve tells me that you are Vice President of Marketing at Keystone Corporation. I am currently National Accounts Manager with Devlin Company and am contemplating a career move into marketing. I would appreciate any information and/or advice that you may have to offer about the best way to make such a transition. What suggestions or ideas could you share with me on this subject?

You: Carl, I have made a recent decision to leave my position as Manager of Corporate Accounting at Wellington Corporation and have begun a job search. I am seeking a position as a Controller of a medium-sized company. I have just begun my job search and was wondering what ideas or suggestions you may have. Martha Barton seemed to feel that you would be a good person to talk with, and that you might have some creative ideas on this subject.

You: Mr. Brighton, I was referred to you by Barbara Wright. Barbara and I are classmates in an O.D. course that we are both taking at the Penn State Graduate Campus. I am currently leaving my position as internal O.D. Consultant at Corning Glass to seek a director level position in a smaller company. As President of the Philadelphia Chapter of the O.D. Network, Barbara feels you are in a unique position to shed some general insight about current developments and opportunities in the O.D. field. What are some of the key developments that you feel would be important for me to consider?

You can readily see from these examples just how easy it is to transition into an employment discussion by asking for general information and/or advice. This kind of very indirect approach is conducive to establishing rapport and getting a good conversation underway concerning your job search. If the networkee is aware of specific opportunities or job leads, there is a high likelihood that this information will be volunteered without your having to ask.

REQUEST FOR NAMES
OF KEY CONTACTS

Whether during the face-to-face informational interview or during the networking phone call, the key to successful networking is securing the names of key contacts. This is the very lifeblood of the networking process and must be accomplished if the employment networking process is to succeed. As a minimum goal, you should strive to secure the names of at least 2 to 3 key contacts from each person you have called or met personally during the networking process. In this way, you assure that your network will continue to expand and eventually lead to that important job opportunity that you seek.

The technique for securing the names of these contacts is fairly simple and straightforward. You simply ask your contact for the names of key persons who may be able to assist you with your job search. These could be either persons who may personally have an interest in your background (potential employers) or individuals who may know such persons (sources).

Generally you should not ask for such leads until the later part of your networking discussion. In this way there is a much better probability that sufficient rapport has been established that the networkee will feel comfortable in sharing names with you. Otherwise, if you request this information prematurely, you may come up empty-handed.

Here are some ways of asking the networkee for the names of key contacts.

You: Ms. Darlington, I really appreciate your sharing your thoughts and suggestions on my job search strategy. This has been very helpful. Before we finish our conversation, however, I'm wondering if you can help me in one additional area. Can you think of the names of some key persons in the industry with whom I should be in contact? These could key industry leaders, consultants, vendors, professors, or others who are knowledgeable about industry developments and may be aware of opportunities. Can you think of 4 or 5 persons whom you would suggest I contact?

You: John, I really appreciate your help. Your general observations about current developments in the industry have been very enlightening. I'm wondering, however, if you can think of others, like yourself, who have a lot of contacts in the industry and would be good for me to talk with. Can you think of the names of a few people whom I might contact?

You: Mr. Rollins, this has been a very helpful conversation, and I really appreciate your time. I would appreciate, though, if you could share your thoughts in one final area. Can you think of other persons who are well known in the food industry, and might be valuable persons for me to contact? Are there 3 or 4 persons you might suggest I contact?

Sometimes, as in the first example, it is helpful to suggest categories of persons for you to contact (industry leaders, consultants, professors, and vendors, for example). By so doing, you are sometimes able to get the networkee to think more broadly. Otherwise, he or she may only be trying to think of persons who might have an interest in personally hiring you. This narrow frame of reference could get in the way of identifying some otherwise important industry contacts who could be of real assistance to you. Should the networkee become "stuck" and not able to think of appropriate contacts, therefore, it may be a good idea to suggest these broader categories of contacts to stimulate more creative thinking on the subject. This technique substantially improves the probability that you will not come up empty-handed.

REQUEST TO USE NAME
AS A REFERRAL

When networking, and asking for the names of key contacts, it is always a good idea to ask the networkee's permission to use his or her name in making contact with their referral. Make sure that they understand that you are simply asking permission to use their name as a "referral," not as a "reference." Obviously, there is a difference, and someone who is unfamiliar with the quality of your work and level of your professionalism would feel most uncomfortable being cited as a reference as opposed to a referral. So, simply ask whether they would mind your using their name in making an introduction to these contacts.

There is a real advantage to using such personal referrals in employment networking. When you mention that you were referred by someone who is known to the person you are contacting, there is a much greater sense of obligation to respond to your needs than if you were making a "cold call" without the benefit of such an introduction.

The following are some suggested ways of requesting approval to use your contacts as referrals.

You: John, I really appreciate your sharing these contacts with me. Would you mind my mentioning to these persons that you suggested I call them? It would be very helpful if I could.

You: Thanks for the names of these key contacts. I really appreciate it. Kathy, would it be okay with you if I mentioned your name when I contact these individuals? This would be very helpful.

You: These contacts will be very helpful to me, and I really appreciate your sharing the names of these persons with me. Would you have any objection if I were to tell these persons that you suggested I call?

"THANK YOU" FOR ASSISTANCE

The final element of an effective networking call is the expression of a simple "thank you" for the assistance that others have given to you. This expression of simple courtesy is just the kind of thing that may cause this contact to call you a day or two later with a couple of more valuable contacts or, even better, an excellent job lead. So, you never know when or how this individual may further impact your life at some future point. A little well-deserved courtesy and a simple "thank you" can well go a long way to cementing a valuable contact and building an important link in your long-term professional network.

9

THE GREAT NETWORKING SHORTCUT

How to Cut 75% From Job Search Time

I n the last two chapters you have been introduced in some detail to the conventional approach to employment networking. Although this approach is known to be highly effective as a job-hunting technique, the key objection to conventional networking is the length of time that it takes to network yourself into a target company and eventually to the target executive who has the authority and power to hire you.

Since networking is the principal job search method by which nearly 70% of all jobs are found, being able to reduce the time necessary to successfully carry out this process has the potential to greatly shorten the time required to conduct a job search. It is the purpose of this chapter to introduce you to such a shortcut. I believe that this shortcut realistically has the potential to reduce job search time by 75% or more.

THE PROBLEM WITH CONVENTIONAL NETWORKING

The way conventional networking is taught to job seekers by reputable outplacement firms is a very indirect, oblique type of process that consumes considerable time in its implementation. On one hand, the job hunter is taught to identify a number of target companies for purposes of the job search. On the other, the job seeker is instructed to identify a huge list of contacts (sometimes several hundred) to begin as the basis for the networking process. It is expected that by networking from this primary contacts list, and proceeding through several levels of subsequent networking contacts (level 1, level 2, level 3, level 4, and so on), sooner or later the job seeker will successfully network into a target company and reach his or her target executive (the person with the authority to hire him or her).

Assuming for the moment that the job hunter has 50 target companies identified, and that it takes on the average of 8 to 10 phone calls to succeed in reaching each targeted executive (a conservative estimate at best), it will take 400 to 500 telephone calls to eventually complete this process. This is an enormously time-consuming process that requires considerable energy and discipline to complete. This, along with other job search activity, can normally translate into several months of job search and a veritable emotional roller coaster ride for the job seeker in the process.

Having personally witnessed numerous persons going through the outplacement process, I have noticed how de-energized and demoralized they can become at about the month to 6-week point in the job search. Despite excellent training in networking skills and techniques, it is very common for a high percentage of persons to reach a sort of "saturation point" at this stage in their search process. Having pretty much exhausted their primary or level 1 contacts (and perhaps their level 2 and level 3 contacts as well), and without much to show for their effort, many job hunters begin to show signs of emotional and physical fatigue.

It is frequently at this stage of the job search, when nothing is happening, that job seekers begin to enter into a period of self-doubt and often experience serious erosion of self-confidence. At this point some serious doubts begin to creep in, and they begin to feel that there is something wrong with them. After all, they have religiously done all they were trained to do, in just the way the outplacement consulting firm has carefully trained them to do it, and... nothing is happening! Therefore they begin to feel that it can't be the process, and there must obviously be something wrong with them. They begin to suspect that they are "not good enough," and these feelings are further reinforced by the lack of positive results from their job-hunting efforts.

At this point in the job search, it is very common for job hunters to experience feelings of depression. They begin to lose confidence and energy, and a period of lethargy frequently sets in. There is a tendency to become somewhat withdrawn, and networking productivity begins to slip considerably. Some will begin to back off networking and begin to pursue the use of more passive, and frequently nonproductive, sources. This further feeds the feelings of frustration and depression.

The results of this kind of "psychological nose-dive" can be quite devastating to the job search process. As energy and productivity begin to drop off and the search begins to lose direction and focus, considerable momentum is lost and the job seeker can unknowingly be tacking several months on to his or her job search time.

It is precisely at this point that an alert, sensitive outplacement counselor will pick up on these symptoms and have a heart-to-heart discussion with his or her client. The thrust of this conversation is to help the client to understand that these feelings of depression are very common at this stage of the search process, and that there is truly nothing wrong with him or her personally. After some re-assurance and comforting, the client is then gently guided back on to the networking track and encouraged to pursue what is known to be a highly successful method for finding jobs.

So, as I'm sure you can see from this scenario, the conventional networking process is a very lengthy and time-consuming one that can take its toll from the emotional standpoint. Job seekers, after several hundred telephone calls, often become tired and depressed, and the resultant loss of energy, self-esteem, and productivity can often add considerable time to the search process.

A MORE DIRECT APPROACH

As previously described, the conventional networking process involves a rather "indirect, oblique" approach to reaching the target company. By starting with a rather large, generalized listing of primary, level 1 contacts at the beginning of the networking process (many of which have no apparent connection with their target companies or target industries, for that matter), outplacement professionals know that it will take the job hunter several levels of networking contact calls to eventually reach a single target executive. This conventional networking process is thus both physically and emotionally fatiguing.

By contrast, what if the job seeker could network directly to his or her target executive in a matter of only 2 or 3 phone calls (versus the 8 or 10 calls normally required by the conventional networking process)? Wouldn't this serve to chop considerable time off the job hunting process, and preserve the energy and self-confidence of the networker? Why, of course it would! So, what are we waiting for? Why not adopt a more focused, direct approach right for the start?

THE NETWORKING SHORTCUT

Several months ago, it occurred to me that it might be a smart idea to apply the research techniques used by executive search firms to the job search networking process. Executive search firms, of course, use these research techniques to systematically identify persons whom they wish to recruit for managerial and executive positions with their client companies. Why couldn't the same research techniques, however, be used by the job seeker to identify the target executives in key target companies as well? Obviously, they can!

By following classical executive search research methodology at the onset of the job search, it is quite possible for the job hunter to identify his or her target executives quickly. In fact, with just 2 or 3 days of carefully planned advance research at the beginning of the job search process, the job seeker can, in fact, identify most (if not all) of the key executives employed by his or her target companies. Also, by putting in place a little bit of additional research, it is possible to identify other persons who are reporting to these target executive as well. These persons, many of which represent peers in the target company, can prove to be a far more effective and efficient source than those typically identified at the target company through conventional networking techniques.

The underlying basis for the planning and execution of a highly effective networking shortcut is the identification of target company functional peers through the use of advance research techniques. By identifying and calling these peers directly, considerable time can be lopped off the traditional networking approach, and you can find yourself talking with your target executive in a matter of 2 or 3 phone calls. In the case cited previously in this chapter (50 target companies), this could mean 50 to 100 phone calls rather than 400 to 500—a time savings of 75% to 90% !

COMPETITIVE ADVANTAGE

In addition to the considerable time savings provided by the networking shortcut approach, there can also be a substantial competitive advantage to be gained from use of this method. Consider the following.

Using the traditional or conventional networking approach, it is not uncommon for the job hunter to network into the target firm through functional areas other than those that have been targeted by the job searcher. For example, although you may be seeking a position in marketing brand management, your initial networking contact at the target company may bring you into the company through the accounting department. Thus, your contacts may lead you to the Corporate Accounting Manager who, in turn, introduces you to the Director of Marketing. This approach does not allow you to gather much information about what is going on in the marketing function of the target company before you find yourself talking directly with the Director of Marketing.

In contrast, by using the networking shortcut that I am recommending, you will have the opportunity to first talk with more junior members of the target firm's marketing department (your peers) before making direct contact with the Director of Marketing. This provides you with the opportunity to gain a considerable amount of strategic information (major marketing problems, new product introductions, brand strategies, pricing issues, quality problems, and so on) before talking with the Director.

Such advance discussion provides you with a substantial competitive advantage over those who make contact with the same Director through conventional networking methods. Before talking with the Director, you already have a great deal of insight concerning the major challenges, problems, and issues with which the Director is currently wrestling. Conventional networking seldom provides the opportunity to gain such advance information and insight.

Instead, you find yourself talking directly with the target executive with little or no insight concerning these important factors.

This advance information and insight should serve you well and provide you with considerable competitive advantage. By carefully guiding subsequent conversation with the Director to areas of major concern, and presenting a few select ideas and suggestions, you may well parlay this initial conversation into a personal, face-to-face meeting (if not an actual employment interview). At very least, if well-orchestrated, this conversation could well serve to solicit excellent job search suggestions or valuable contacts that will prove useful to your job-hunting campaign.

HOW TO USE EXECUTIVE SEARCH RESEARCH TECHNIQUES

The underlying basis for shortcutting the conventional networking process, as previously discussed, is the advance research done at the beginning of the networking process. To save valuable job search time and maximize results, however, this research should be undertaken immediately following the preparation of your resume and completion of your executive search firm/employment agency mail campaign (see Chapter 4).

As noted earlier in this book, it is important to first complete the executive search/employment agency mail campaign since this will be "out there working" at the same time you are carrying out your employment networking program. In this way, you will have two major job search efforts working simultaneously, which should serve to surface more job opportunities sooner—thus expediting your job search.

There are two basic steps required in the networking shortcut research process:

1. Identification of target companies

2. Identification of target executives

The specific processes for carrying out these two steps in the research method are very similar. Let's examine the processes for both of these research steps.

Identifying Target Companies

Target companies, as you already know, are defined as those key companies, within your target industries, for whom you would like to work. They include all such companies that have facilities and job opportunities within your target geography (those geographical areas that you have targeted for job search purposes).

The first step in the networking shortcut research process, therefore, becomes the systematic identification of these target companies.

There are a couple of key reference sources that can be used to help you to systematically identify target companies. These references are the very "Bibles" of the executive search profession, and are used routinely by retained executive search firms for the same purpose. These key references are as follows:

1. *Encyclopedia of Associations.* This Encyclopedia, published by Gale Research in Detroit, Michigan, contains complete descriptions of over 25,000 associations. These include trade, business, and commercial associations that are associated with specific industry groupings. A topical or subject index is provided to facilitate identification of key associations related to your target industries. Most of these trade or industry associations publish a directory which lists member companies, which may be available to you upon request.

2. *Directories in Print.* Also published by Gale Research, this two-volume encyclopedia is an annotated guide to over 10,000 business, industrial, professional and other directories that are published in the United States. A topical or subject index allows you to quickly identify industry directories related to your job search. Many of these provide a comprehensive list of companies that are members of a particular industry grouping.

3. *Thomas Register of American Manufacturers.* Published by the Thomas Publishing Company in New York City, the register is a multivolume encyclopedia that lists thousands of U.S. manufacturers. The first seven volumes provide a comprehensive alphabetical listing of products and services, along with the hundreds of companies who manufacture or provide them. Obviously, this encyclopedia can be used as a supplemental reference source to the two reference sources already described.

The specific research process used to identify the names, addresses, and telephone numbers of target companies (and sometimes target executives as well) is as follows:

1. Using the *Encyclopedia of Associations*, identify the industry/trade associations to which members of your target industries belong.

2. Contact the officers of these key associations to determine what industry directories exist that list all (or most) of the companies that are members of the target industry. (Note: These may be published directly by the association or by a private publisher. Officers of the association are usually very aware of such publications, however, and will advise you accordingly.)
    Where appropriate, secure such industry directories and research them for the names, addresses, and tele-

phone numbers of those companies you wish to target for your job search. (Note: Sometimes the names and titles of key target executives are available as well.)

3. Use the *Directories in Print* as a cross-reference to the recommendations made by the trade/industry association office. Where appropriate, order additional industry directories shown in this directory.

4. Use the *Thomas Register of American Manufacturers* as a further cross-reference to identify additional companies not listed in the directories secured through your previous research.

5. Consolidate and prepare a final listing of all key companies you wish to include on your target list. Include company name, address, and phone number (also, name and title of key target executive—if available).

Since you are looking to minimize the time needed to conduct your job search, it is suggested that you order these directories by telephone using a credit card. Likewise, you can request that the publisher send the directory to your attention using Federal Express overnight delivery, charging these Federal Express charges to your credit card as well. Where use of a credit card is unacceptable and the publisher requires payment by check, you can use Federal Express to send both your order and check to the publisher on an overnight basis. With advance agreement of the publisher, you may be able to increase the amount of your check to include the cost of return Federal Express and have the directory delivered to you the day following receipt of your order by the publisher.

If you have followed the research procedures provided in this section of the chapter, it is likely that you have been able to put together a fairly comprehensive listing of firms in your target industries, and are now ready to move on to the identification of target executives for each. The process for doing this is fairly similar to that which you have just used to identify target companies.

Identifying Target Executives (and Peers)

Target executives, as you are aware from previous discussion, are defined as those executives who work for your target companies, are responsible for management of the functional areas you have targeted for employment, and who have the authority to hire you. The second step in the networking shortcut research process, therefore, is to systematically identify these key executives.

Some of the same key reference sources that you have used to identify target companies can also be used for the identification of target executives. Likewise, these same references are also used as key research sources by retained executive search firms for identification of target executives. These references include:

1. *Encyclopedia of Associations*

2. *Directories in Print*

The specific research process to be used by you to identify the names and titles of target executives for your job search is as follows:

1. Using the *Encyclopedia of Associations*, identify the professional associations to which members of your target executive group will likely belong. (Such associations are normally related to the functional areas you have targeted for your search—marketing, accounting, human resources, manufacturing, and so on.)

2. Contact the officers of these key professional associations to determine what directories exist that list many

(or all) of your target executive group. (Note: Such directories may be published directly by the professional association itself, or may be published by other sources. Association officers, however, are frequently knowledgeable of the existence of such directories and can tell you how to acquire them. Additionally, if published by the professional association itself, sometimes distribution of these directories is limited only to members of the association and cannot be acquired by the general public. In such cases your options are to join the association or to quietly borrow the directory from an association member.)

3. Use the *Directories in Print* as a cross-reference to the recommendations made by the professional association offices. Where appropriate, order additional professional directories found in this directory to supplement those already on order.

If your target executives are at the corporate officer level, it may be easier and faster to research the names of these executives using one or more of the following reference sources:

1. *Standard & Poor's Register of Corporations, Directors and Executives*

2. *Dun & Bradstreet Million Dollar Directory*

3. *Dun & Bradstreet Reference Book of Corporate Managements*

4. *Standard Directory of Advertisers and Supplements*

5. *Thomas Register of American Manufacturers*

When reviewing these various directories, especially those from the professional and trade associations, it is important to remember to target peer-level personnel as well.

This will provide you with the names, titles, and telephone numbers of those to whom you will want to network first, before contacting your key target executives. Without these preliminary networking calls, you will lose the competitive advantage that can be realized by first gaining some strategic insight into the function that you have targeted for your job search. Therefore, identification of these peer-level individuals will be very important to the overall effectiveness of your networking process.

If you have carefully followed the research procedures recommended above, you should be successful in identifying a fairly complete list of both target executives and peer-level personnel from your target companies. The next step in the process is to make networking calls to the peers that you have identified during your advance research.

It should be pointed out that some of these directories can be rather expensive. Where this is the case, therefore, you may find that copies of the industry directories are available for your free use at the libraries of some of the member companies whose corporate offices are located close by. Additionally, it may be possible to borrow copies of professional association membership directories from local members or regional officers of these associations.

NETWORKING THROUGH TARGET COMPANY PEERS

Where a number of your target company peers are members of certain professional associations, you may find it beneficial to join these associations. Doing so allows you to introduce yourself as a "fellow member" of the professional association. Such a reference, if handled well, can help to establish a professional bond and sense of personal commitment toward helping you that might not otherwise be achieved through a "cold call" to the same individuals.

When networking through your peer group, you must be careful not to overplay the professional association connection. If this comes across as too shallow, and it appears that you have joined the association for the sole purpose of conducting your job search, you stand the chance of turning some of these valuable contacts off. Good judgment and sensitivity need to prevail if you are to optimize this important networking opportunity.

The ground rules for this kind of networking are similar to those discussed in detail in Chapter 8. They are as follows:

1. Use an "indirect" versus a "direct" approach.

2. Never ask directly for a job or job leads.

3. Instead, ask for information and/or advice that will be helpful to your job search, for instance:
   a. Suggestions/advice concerning your job search strategy
   b. Information regarding your target industry and/or target companies
   c. Names of key contacts
   d. Introduction to key contacts

Using this softer, indirect approach will encourage the networkee to open up and share valuable information with you. Normally, if your contact is aware of specific jobs or job leads, this kind of indirect approach will cause him or her to volunteer this information in an effort to be helpful.

Toward the end of your networking call, you will want to direct the conversation back toward the networkee's employer (one of your target companies). The following are some transitional statements that may help you to accomplish this:

Transition # 1

You: Thanks, John, I really appreciate the contacts and know that they will be very helpful to me in my job search. Before I leave, however, I'm wondering if you might share some insight about what is happening there in the marketing department at Reardon Company. I was planning to give Terry Jones (the Director of Marketing) a call, and it would be helpful to have some insight about your business before doing so. Would you mind sharing some observations with me?

Peer: No. What did you have in mind?

You: It would be helpful to learn a little about some of the key problems and challenges currently being faced by your marketing department, as well as some general information about some of the major changes you are trying to bring about. I would, of course, want to avoid any sensitive or proprietary areas, so that I don't put you on the spot. What seem to be some of the department's key challenges?

Peer: Well, for one, we have been steadily losing market share in our frozen food brands. In the last year, for example, our Chicken Little line has lost nearly 22%. No one is quite sure why this is.

You: What do you feel is causing this?

Peer: I'm not really sure, but I believe it may have something to do with quality. Sales have fallen off a bit ever since we changed the recipe last March.

You: I see. Have other frozen food recipes been changed as well?

Peer: Yes. We had a new Flavor Specialist come in last year, and several of our recipes have since been changed.

You: Has any consumer testing been done on the products that have been changed?

Peer: Not really!

You: I see. What are some of the major challenges you are facing?

Peer: We are attempting to reposition our Lady Tillary brand of frozen vegetables on the high price end of the market by changing packaging and improving the quality of our vegetables.

Transition # 2

You: John, I really appreciate your help. I'm wondering, however, if you could take a few minutes and tell me a little about Reardon Company? I was planning to give Terry Jones a call, and a quick overview would be quite helpful.

Peer: What did you have in mind?

You: I would be interested in a broad overview of the major issues and challenges facing the marketing function at Reardon. What can you tell me, John?

Peer: Well, it seems that our single greatest challenge is trying to find a way to stop the hemorrhaging of our best-selling brand, Gleam Max. In the last two years, four of our major competitors have introduced floor waxes as good as or better than Gleam. We have witnessed enormous erosion of our market share, from 65% to less than 20%...

As you can see from these sample networking calls, there is considerable competitive advantage to be gained by first networking through peers before approaching your target executive. Clearly, those using conventional networking techniques are at a distinct disadvantage in not having access to the kind of information gleaned by the job seeker using the networking shortcut described here.

NETWORKING THROUGH TARGET EXECUTIVES

When employing the networking shortcut described in this chapter, your introduction to the target executive will now play off of the previous conversation that you have had with that executive's subordinate. Here are some sample introductory statements that you might employ.

You: Good morning, Mr. Jones, this is Barbara Paxton calling. David Weller (your previous networking contact) and I are fellow members of the American Marketing Association and I am calling you for some advice and suggestions concerning a career change that I am currently contemplating. David says that you are very knowledgeable and have a number of contacts in the industry. Is this a convenient time for you to talk with me?

You: Ms. Lorton, this is Carl Richardson calling. During a conversation that Linda Franklin (your prior peer-level contact and Lorton's subordinate) and I were having the other day, she mentioned that you are extremely knowledgeable and know a lot of persons in the food industry. Linda and I are fellow members of the American Marketing Association. Ms. Lorton, I am in the process of leaving my position as Brand Manager at Garring Corporation, and would appreciate your advice and suggestions concerning my job search strategy. Is this a convenient time for you to talk?

You will note in these examples how it is possible to introduce the name of the target executive's subordinate into the introduction by simply alluding to your prior conversation with the subordinate and a reference to the fact that you are both members of the same professional association. Both of these factors are valid references, but the target executive has no way of knowing just how strong a relationship you may have with the subordinate. There is thus an implied professional obligation for the target executive to respond to your request for job search advice and assistance.

The balance of the networking approach used by you should make full use of the methods and techniques already discussed in detail in Chapter 8. I do not wish to be redundant by repeating them here.

As you can see, the networking shortcut, if properly used, can be highly effective and can serve to cut considerable time from your job search. In some cases, if used effectively, this technique can help you to shave 75% to 90% off the networking process. Since networking accounts for approximately 70% of all jobs found by the average job seeker, this could mean a significant savings in the overall time needed to conduct a successful job-hunting campaign. Certainly, it could prove to be a highly effective technique in supporting the goal of completing your job search within the 60-day time frame.

10

POWER STRATEGIES
FOR SUCCESSFUL
INTERVIEWS

G enerating employment interviews through the effective use of key employment sources (networking, search firms/employment agencies, and advertising) is one thing; landing a job offer is quite another.
If you are going to be successful in completing your job
search within a reasonable time frame, therefore, you will
need to become proficient in the art and science of interviewing.

Although this is primarily a book on employment
sources, and how to use them, I would be remiss in not
at least sharing with you a few interview secrets that could
strengthen your interview effectiveness considerably. If you
are looking for more in-depth help with building your interview skills and preparing for the interview, I suggest that
you read my book on interviewing (*The Five-Minute Interview*), which is likely available through your local bookstore or library.

Interviewing as an employment candidate is something that simply does not come naturally to the great majority of us. I have never ceased to be amazed at the number of otherwise highly articulate and highly seasoned senior level executives who seem like fish out of water during the employment interview, when they are on the side of the table where they have to answer the questions. I suppose that each of us has at least a small degree of anxiety about this particular event.

I have long been both a student and a teacher of interviewing techniques. I continually observe new techniques and trends, always looking for a better way to do it—both from the interviewee's and the employer's side of the interview equation. Occasionally I discover something new and stimulating that is worth passing on to others. These observations are the basis for this chapter on power strategies for successful interviews.

KEY INTERVIEW STRATEGIES

Over the years as an interviewer for both a major *Fortune* 200 company (I was the Manager of Technical Employment for the Scott Paper Company) and my own human resources consulting firm, the Brandywine Consulting Group (where I carry out retained executive search assignments for client companies), I have observed some specific techniques that have proven to be particularly effective when used by interviewees. Whether or not the candidates who used them thought of them in the context of interview strategies, I'm not sure. However, what I do know is that, when effectively employed, these strategies (or techniques) can have an extremely positive impact on employment decision makers and are worthy of your attention.

These interview strategies were derived from my participation, as interviewer, in better than 2,000 interviews during my professional career. They are techniques that I have actually seen candidates use, and I was sufficiently impressed to take special note of them. Although there are no formal names for these methods, I have given them names as follows:

1. The strategic change strategy

2. The performance deficit strategy

3. The ideal candidate strategy

4. The key problems/challenges strategy

All of these strategies have one important thing in common. They are all aimed at finding what the employer is "buying." Each is aimed at finding out exactly what is important to the hiring manager, to whom the employment candidate would be reporting.

WHERE INTERVIEWS GO AGROUND

Most interviews go aground and begin to sink when the candidate (the interviewee) fails to focus on those things that are important to the hiring manager (his or her prospective boss). This is not dissimilar to a sales person who fails to pay attention to what the buyer is thinking.

Sometimes a sales person can provide an outstanding sales presentation and still walk away from the sale without an order. He or she can spend hours extolling the virtues of the product, speaking at great length about all of the product's uses and attributes, but unless the sales person discovers what specific factors will motivate the customer to buy, he or she may waste considerable time talking about attributes that are of little or no importance to the buyer. The result is—no sale!

There is a direct parallel that can be drawn between selling and the interview strategy. I have often observed interviewees drone on for hours about their skills, capabilities, experience, qualifications, and so on, never once pausing to ask what it was the hiring manager was really looking for. The result was the same as with the unlucky sales person—no offer!

My advice to you, then, is take time to smell the roses. Pause in your interview discussion to take time to carefully probe what it is the employer is looking for. What is it that will get that hiring manager excited about a candidate? What is the hiring manager really buying?

The strategies mentioned above will help you to do exactly that. They will provide you with the tools to carefully extract and define those factors that are truly important to the hiring manager's employment decision. Let's take a look at each of these power strategies, so that you can be more appreciative of their potential in helping you to come out of the interview process as a winner.

THE STRATEGIC CHANGE STRATEGY

One key power strategy for winning the interview is known as the strategic change strategy. The basis for this strategy is that all hiring managers, regardless of who they are, are looking for help in achieving their strategic goals. The purpose of this strategy is, therefore, to discover the specific strategic changes that the employer is looking to drive, and then to bill yourself as a "change agent"—one who can bring these important changes about.

The technique for using this strategy is to ask the hiring manager (preferably early in the interview) about the organization's strategic goals. Specifically, what are the major changes that the hiring manager will need to make, and what are the key problems that will need to be solved in order to bring these changes about?

These are some of the questions that you will need to ask of the hiring manager, if you are to effectively use this strategy. By discovering these strategic problems early in the interview discussion, you have the opportunity to return to these problems (later in the interview), after you have had time to think about them in a quality way, and talk about your ability to help solve these key problems and assist the manager in achieving his or her objectives.

Here is a suggested way of positioning yourself to probe this area and get the information you need to carry out this strategy.

You: Mr. Jackson, tell me a little about some of your business strategy for this department. What are some of the major strategic changes you would like to bring about, and why are these important to you?

THE PERFORMANCE DEFICIT STRATEGY

Most conscientious managers are never completely satisfied with the overall performance of their organizations. They are always looking to bring about continual improvement to their functions. The focus of this strategy is to discover exactly where the hiring manager would like to see performance improvement brought about.

The following is an example of a line of inquiry that you can use to find out what these improvement needs are:

You: Ms. Showalter, as you think about the position for which I am interviewing, what aspects of this job would you like to see performed better? What kind of improvement would you like to see?

Here is another opportunity for you to shine in the interview. By suggesting ways in which you can help Ms. Showalter to improve performance in these important areas, you increase the probability of generating some real interest in your employment candidacy.

THE IDEAL CANDIDATE
STRATEGY

I have always been amazed to find how few interviewees are aware of this powerful interview technique. Basically, it is a very direct approach to finding out what the hiring manager is looking for, by simply asking. Here is how you can implement this strategy by asking the hiring manager one or two very basic questions.

You: Jim what are you really looking for here? How would you describe the ideal candidate for this position?

The answer to this one will provide you with a significant competitive advantage in the interview. Now you know exactly what the hiring manager is seeking. Your mission now becomes to convince him or her that you have the specific traits and qualifications sought.

THE KEY PROBLEMS
AND CHALLENGES STRATEGY

When you reduce employment to its very basics, the fact of the matter is that hiring takes place because of the need to solve problems. That is truly what each of us is paid for—to solve particular problems and move the business ahead. The more complex the problems, usually the higher the pay.

As an employment candidate, then, it makes good sense to find out what the key problems are that you will be called upon to solve.

Here is a technique that will help you to explore this important area as part of your overall interview strategy:

You: Mr. Wells, what do you consider the key problems and challenges of this position? Which of these do you consider the most important, and why?

Here again, you have a unique opportunity to focus the interview discussion on areas of the position (and your qualifications) that are of interest to the hiring manager.

SUMMARY

As you can see, all of these can truly be power interview strategies if effectively used. They enable you to gain a great deal of insight into what the hiring manager is "buying" and provide you with the opportunity for significant competitive advantage in the interview. Few of the other candidates, with whom you will be competing, will think to use these particular strategies, and you will gain a real competitive edge by doing so.

INDEX

ACCESS, 55–56
Advertising, 5, 15–16, 18
  alternative ways to use publications,
    72–73
  Ben Franklin balance sheet
    approach, 74
  cover letters responding to, 74–78
  geographical saturation, 68
  linear comparison approach, 75
  market segments, 65
  maximizing the use of, as a job
    search source, 63, 65
  narrative comparison approach, 75
  national market, 65, 66–69
  percentage of jobs found through,
    13, 18, 63
  as a productive job search source, 12
  to a professional specialty, 65, 71–72
  in recruitment of blue collar workers,
    15–16
  regional, 68, 70
  response, 73
  saturation strategy, 64–66
  target geography, 65, 66, 69–70
  target industry, 65, 70–71
  when to read recruitment ads, 64
AESC Membership Directory, 56
Alumni placement offices, 6, 9
American Business Directories, Inc., 57
American Management Association, 58
Association of Executive Search
    Consultants (AESC), 56
Attorneys, 5, 146

Bank officers, 5, 146
Beatty Study, 10–14, 17–18
Ben Franklin balance sheet approach,
  74
Big 3 job search sources, 6, 10, 12, 16,
  19, 64
Blue collar jobs, 15–16, 83
Bob Adams, Inc., 57–58
Brandywine Consulting Group, 189
Bureau of Labor Statistics Bulletin
  #1866, 15, 83
Business consultants, 5
Business contacts, 146

Capital venture firms, 5
Career consultants, 5
Career continuity, 25, 27, 28, 29
Career objective, 26
Career progression, 25, 26, 27, 28
Career stagnation, 29
Carter, Joseph, 84–86
Challenger, Gray & Christmas, 13, 80,
  81
Challenger, Jim, 13
Change agent, job seeker as, 191
Chronological resume, 23. *See also*
    Linear resume
  advantages, 25
  characteristics, 24–25
  classical, 32, 34–35
  disadvantages, 25–26
  samples of, 32–33, 34–39
Classical chronological resume, 32,
  34–35
Cold calls, 104, 138, 155, 167, 182
Community contacts, 145
Company expansions, 73
Computer job banks, 5
Computer resume matching services, 9
Contingency employment agencies, 49.
    See also Employment agencies
Contingent fee, 50
Cover letters:
  components of advertising response
    letter, 76–78
  to executive search firms, 59–60
  in response to advertising, 74–76
  samples of, 77, 78

Department of Labor Study, 13, 14–16,
  83
Direct mail to employers, 5, 46
  as a productive job search source, 9,
    12
Direct mail to executive search
    firms/employment agencies, 45,
    175
  cautions concerning, 48
  components of cover letter, 59–61
  components of mailing, 59–61
  developing the mailing list, 54–55

Direct mail to executive search
    firms/employment agencies *cont.*
    distinguishing search firms from
        employment agencies, 49–52
    expected results of, 47–48
    for outplacement, 47
    response rate, 47, 58
    sample cover letter, 60
    size of mailing, 58
    sources for mailing list, 55–58
    targeting the right firms, 48–49
Directories in Print, 177, 178, 179, 180
Directory of Executive Recruiters, 56
Downsizing, 10, 132, 133, 134, 156
Drake Beam Morin, 80, 81
*Dun & Bradstreet Million Dollar
    Directory*, 180
*Dun & Bradstreet Reference Book of
    Corporate Managements*, 180

Educational contacts, 145
Employee referral programs, 5
Employment agencies, 5
    compared to outplacement
        consulting firms, 11
    contingency, 49
    distinguished from executive search
        firms, 49–52
    fees, 51–52
    percentage of jobs found through,
        13, 18
    as a productive job search source,
        12
    selection guidelines, 53–54
    types of positions filled by, 52
Employment studies, 6, 9–10
    Beatty and Department of Labor
        studies compared, 14
    Beatty and Granovetter studies
        compared, 17–18
    Beatty Study, 10–14
    combined results of, 18–19
    key message from, 19–20
    statistics on networking as a job
        search source, 80–83
Encyclopedia of Associations, 70, 72,
    176, 177, 179
Executive Assets Corporation, 80, 81
Executive Employment Guide, 58
Executive Search Consultants, 57
Executive search firms, 5, 16, 18
    blue chip, 51, 56
    direct mail campaign to, 47
    distinguished from employment
        agencies, 49–52
    fees, 50–51

percentage of jobs found through,
    13, 18
as a productive job search source,
    12, 16
retained, 49
selection guidelines for, 53
types of positions filled by, 51
Expanding companies, 73

Fear, 136–139
Functional resume, 23
    advantages, 27
    characteristics, 26–27
    disadvantages, 28
    functions-based, 33, 40–41
    samples of, 33, 40–43
    when to use, 29–30
Functions-based functional resume,
    33, 40–41

Geographical saturation, 68
Granovetter, Mark S., 16, 142
Granovetter Study, 13, 16–18, 82–83

Hidden job market, 142–143
Hybrid job search firms, 52
    guidelines for selecting, 53
    types of positions filled by, 52

Ideal candidate interview strategy, 192
Industry associations, 5.
    See also Trade associations
Informational interviews, 160–163
Interviews:
    failure in, 189–190
    ideal candidate strategy, 192
    informational, 160–163
    key problems and challenges
        strategy, 193
    performance deficit strategy,
        191–192
    power strategies for, 188–189, 193
    resume as a focal point in, 22
    strategic change strategy, 190–191

Janotta Bray and Associates, 80, 81
*Job Bank Guide to Employment
    Services*, 57–58
Job fairs, 5
Job hopping, 26, 27, 28, 29
Job market, segments of, 65
Job offer negotiations, 11
Job search:
    barriers to effective, 4
    informal methods of, 15, 17
    jump starting, 45

misinformation about, 3–4
saturation point in, 170
self-doubt and, 171–172
timing in, 6–7
training for, 11, 12
trial-and-error approach to, 4
Job search sources:
advertising as, 12, 13, 18, 63
Big 3, 6, 10, 12, 16, 19, 64
for blue collar vs. white collar jobs, 15–16
eliminating nonproductive, 3
fully exploiting, 3, 6
identifying the best, 2, 5–6, 9
partial list of, 5–6
prioritizing the best, 3
studies of, 6, 9–20.
See also Employment studies
Job stability, 25

Kennedy & Kennedy, Inc., 56
Key contacts, 165–167
Key problems and challenges interview strategy, 193
King Chapman & Broussard, Inc., 80, 81, 87–88

Layoffs, 134
Lee Hecht Harrison, Inc., 80, 81, 89
Linear comparison approach, 74, 75
Linear resume, 23
advantages over classical chronological, 32–33
samples of, 36–39
Lord, Virginia M., 86–87

Mainstream Access, 80, 81
Manchester, 80, 81, 84
Misinformation, 3–4

Narrative comparison approach, 74, 75
Narrative linear resume, 32, 38–39
National Ad Search, The, 68, 69
National Association of Personnel Consultants, 55–56
National Business Employment Weekly, 68, 69
National market, 65, 66–69
Networking, 5
competitive advantage in, 143
credibility and, 141
defined, 79, 89
Department of Labor Study of, 82, 83
deterrents to use of, 131–132
expert opinions about, 83–90
as an exponential process, 139–140

with friends, 86, 133, 144, 147
Granovetter Study of, 82–83
and the hidden job market, 142–143
mathematical progression of, 140
a more direct approach to, 172
newly created jobs, 82, 142
objective of, 143–144
percentage of jobs found through, 13, 18, 135
primary contact list, 145–146
prioritization of contacts, 146–147
problems with conventional, 169, 170–172, 174–175
as a productive job search source, 12, 16, 79, 81, 87, 88, 131, 139–141
rejection, 138
role of, in job search, 79
sense of obligation in, 140–141
shortcut to, 173–186
survey of outplacement firms concerning, 10–14, 80–81
timing of, 64
using executive search research techniques, 175–181
Networking phone call:
asking for advice *vs.* asking for a job, 153, 162–163
background summary, 157–160
dealing with fear, 136–139
expressing the purpose of, 152–155
expressing thank you for assistance, 168
introduction, 148–150
key elements of, 148
overcoming embarrassment, 132–135
request for information and advice, 163–164
request for names of key contacts, 165-167
request for personal meeting, 160–163
request to use name for referral, 167–168
small talk, 151–152
specific requests for assistance, 160
stating name and relationship of referral, 150–151, 155
suggested approach to, 85–86
volunteering the reason for availability, 155–157
warm-up calls to friends, 147
Networking shortcut, 173
competitive advantage of, 174–175, 181, 184
identifying target companies, 85, 176–179

Networking shortcut, (*cont.*)
  identifying target executives and
    peers, 179–180
  networking through target company
    peers, 144, 170, 181–184
  networking through target
    executives, 144, 185–186
  steps in, 176
New hire announcements, 73
Newly created jobs, 82, 142

Obituary notices, 73
Outplacement consulting firms:
  assistance provided by, 11
  compared to employment agencies,
    11–12
  defined, 10
  direct mail campaign to, 47
  survey of, 10–14, 80–81

Performance deficit interview strategy,
  191–192
Personal contact, *see* Networking
Personal referrals, 105, 141
Primary (level 1) contacts list,
  145–146, 170, 172
  prioritization of, 146–147
Professional associations, 5, 72, 85,
  144, 146, 180, 181, 186
Professional specialty, 65, 71–72
Promotional announcements, 73

Recruitment advertising,
  See Advertising
Resume:
  appearance of, 30–31
  as a focal point during interviews, 22
  as a marketing tool, 21–22
  reference value of, 22–23
  samples of, 32–43
  selecting the right type, 24, 29–30
  and success of job hunting
    campaign, 21–23
  types of, 23
Retained executive search firm, 49, 50.
  See also Executive search firm
Retainer fee, 50
Reverse chronological resume, 25
Right Associates, 80, 81, 86
Ross, Ronald S., 87–88

Saturation bombing, 65
Search firms, *See* Executive search
  firms
Secretaries:
  befriending, 93–94
  call backs, 128–130

fourth stage barriers, 116–128
as gatekeeper, 92
as helper/facilitator, 92–93, 128
keys to an effective relationship
  with, 94–95
overcoming common barriers and
  objections, 96
responding to executive not available
  barrier, 97–104
responding to questions about
  reason for call, 109–116
responding to questions about
  relationship with his/her boss,
  104–109
role of, 91–93
smiling over the phone, 95–96
60-day concept of job hunting:
  proven success of, 1, 4
  underlying principles of, 2–3, 7–8
Skills-based functional resume, 33,
  42–43
Smiling, 95–96
Social contacts, 145
Sourcing calls, 138
Spanier, Sheryl, 89–90
Specialty publications, 70–71
*Standard & Poor's Directory of
  Advertisers and Supplements*,
  180
*Standard & Poor's Register of
  Corporations, Directors and
  Executives*, 180
State employment service, 5
Straight linear resume, 32, 36–37
Strategic change interview strategy,
  190–191

Target company peers, 181–184
  ground rules for networking with,
  182
Target executives, 144, 170, 179–180
Target geography, 65, 66, 69–70, 176
Target industry, 65, 70–71
*Thomas Register of American
  Manufacturers*, 177, 178, 179,
  180
Timing, 6–7
Trade associations, 5, 65, 70, 146, 176
Training, 11, 12
Trial-and-error approach to job
  hunting, 4
Troubled companies, 73, 176–179
2-minute drill, 157–160
Unconventional resumes, 24
Underemployment, 26, 28, 30
Unemployment, 3, 27, 28, 29, 133,
  134